paint a poem

Moira Andrew

Line drawings by Andrea Heath

Acknowledgements

The author and publishers would like to give special thanks to the staff of Dinas Powys Infants School, Vale of Glamorgan, and Malpas Church Junior School, Newport, for their generous help and support during the preparation of *Paint a Poem*. They also wish to thank the children of these schools for their many contributions of poetry and artwork. Our thanks are due also to the children in the author's tutor groups who have taken part in the Pearse House Lending Our Minds Out residential writing courses over the years.

They would like to thank Abertillery Primary School; Albert Road School, Penarth; Mount Street Junior School, Brecon; Pendoylan Church in Wales Primary School; Llansannor Church in Wales Primary School, and Franksbridge County Primary School for their contributions to the children's work in this book; and Lucy Allen and James Allen for the cover artwork.

The author and publishers wish to thank Wes Magee for permission to use his poem, 'A week of winter weather', first published in The Witch's Brew and other poems, OUP, 1989.

The publishers would also like to thank Moira Andrew for inclusion of copyright material as follows: 'Poems aren't all that difficult' and 'New nursery rhyme' first published in *Through a window* by Longman, 1995; 'On the skyline' first published by Nelson, 1993; 'Letter from Egypt' first published by CUP, 1992; 'Power' and 'Weather Wheel' first published by Stanley Thornes, 1995; and 'Raspberry jam' first published in *A Shooting Star* (poems collected by Wes Magee) by Blackwell, 1985.

Weather Wheel

(Start at any point and read clockwise)

by Moira Andrew

See Weather Wheel, page 60

First published in 1996 by BELAIR PUBLICATIONS LIMITED
Apex Business Centre, Boscombe Road, Dunstable, LU5 4RL, United Kingdom

Reprinted 1998, 1999, 2000, 2001.

Series editor: Robyn Gordon Design: Lynn Hooker Photography: Kelvin Freeman Line drawings: Andrea Heath

ISBN: 0 94788 244-8

Contents

APPROACHES

Poetry can be a magic experience for everyone. To make such experience possible for children, it is crucial that they are given opportunities, not only to read widely and to write their own poems, but to listen to all kinds of poetry being read aloud - that way lies enchantment.

LISTENING

Nursery rhymes are often a young child's introduction to the world of poetry. Extend these sessions to include finger-plays, songs and poems of all kinds. Let them join in, make up new rhymes, talk about the poems, dramatise them, and paint or draw some of the characters.
However, listening should not stop with the five to seven-year-olds. Older children should be encouraged to take an active part in poetry-reading/listening sessions, sometimes in small groups, sometimes as a whole school. Active listening implies questioning, choosing and making judgements about the poems - and indeed, about the poets!
These sessions should be as interesting and exciting as possible. Introduce a variety of styles: narrative and conversation poems; poems to make children think deeply, feel sad perhaps; rhyming and non-rhyming poems; poems to make everyone laugh out loud! Read and re-read favourite poems until the children are able to build up an anthology in their heads.

READING

A variety of collections and anthologies should be readily accessible to the children so that they can find their favourite poems, see the pattern the words make on the page, and discover new poems to enjoy reading for themselves.

TEACHING STRATEGIES

It is important to explore a variety of teaching strategies to give children success, because in success lies enjoyment.

Word trading

When you act as scribe for the children (putting a poem together on a flip chart or board from the children's own suggestions), don't simply take the first suitable word they come up with, but 'trade words' with them. Add word on word until they build into a toppling mountain of language. For example, the children may suggest that a lost child will feel *scared, desperate, frightened, terrified, cold, lonely, nightmarish, panic-stricken*, and so on. In describing how a dragonfly moves, even the youngest children may go from the ordinary *flying* to *swooping, soaring, hovering, gliding, floating*....such richness!
Time spent on oral work of this kind makes the point that language is a flexible, exciting, living thing, full of possibilities; that no two poems will every be quite the same; that a poet never stops playing with words.

'Going shopping' for a poem

A shopping list is such a mundane thing that this approach takes some of the mystique out of writing poetry and gives every child a starting point.

Begin with a word-trading session, gathering as many ideas as possible. Then choose only two words from those that the children have suggested to make a class 'shopping list' on the board. When the children move on to their individual work, encourage them to use the 'borrow one, find one' rule. That is, that they may borrow one word from the class list, but must find a second (original) one for themselves. Allowing children to borrow words gives a feeling of confidence to any who need it.

It is important to have a writing table which is easily accessible to the children. This should be equipped with a range of plain and coloured papers, pencils, crayon pencils, safety scissors, etc. Beside this, it is useful to place a table of 'inspirations' displaying picture books, music tapes, shells, plants and so on **(see photograph).**

Encourage the children to use scrap paper or a rough book to make a shopping list *before* they begin to tackle the poem. With the shopping list on the left-hand page, the children can use this as a basis for their rough work, ticking off each idea as they go along.

From rough to best

Going from rough work to best work gives the children a working strategy. Impress on them that, at the rough stage, handwriting and spelling are of secondary importance. Drafting, that is getting words and ideas on paper, is the task in hand. Show children that they can cross out, use arrows and try again - 'rough work' means what it says!

This stage also gives teachers the opportunity to act as editors, asking questions of the children and commenting on what they have written. It is a time for encouragement and appreciation.

PRESENTATION

Final presentation should be as polished as the children can make it. Poetry is for sharing, so they should be encouraged to think of audience at this stage. Is the poem to be displayed on the classroom wall or published in an anthology? Either way, spelling should be correct, handwriting clear and legible, and word-processed work should be well laid out.

An attractive display of poetry, arranged with obvious care, adds much to the ambience of the classroom and demonstrates to the children that their work is valued by the adults in their world.

There are other ways of presenting poetry, of course. Sometimes poems are best performed before an audience of parents or other children in the school. Poems can be put on tape, perhaps set to music. They can be produced as poetry posters, published as one-poem books or riddles.

Discuss with the children their ideas for presentation. Some may be unworkable, others too time-consuming, but many of their ideas will be exciting and highly creative - perhaps reflecting much of the originality and flair of their writing.

BASIC IMAGE

The ability to use image, to make connections between one idea and another, is where poetry begins. 'Image' is shorthand for simile and metaphor, and is a useful way of describing this way of thinking to very young children. They all know about their imaginations, how they can 'make pictures' in their heads, so they can understand something of what is meant by the word *image*.

THE MAGIC HAT

To introduce the idea of using image to the very youngest children, sit them in a library corner and suggest that they each put on a magic hat. This hat is so magic that it is invisible! Get them to place the invisible hat on their head. Now they can see pictures in a new and special way.

Show a picture of a cloud, a rainbow, sheep in a field, a winter tree - even a washing maching! (See 'Poems aren't all that difficult', below.) Wearing the magic hat, the children will be able to see the picture in a different way: for example, clouds can look like pillows, cobwebs, marshmallows, grumpy faces; a rainbow like an umbrella, a mushroom, a slide, a bridge, a sad face, and so on. Encourage the children to think of as many different and exciting ideas as they can. It is the beginning of 'thinking like a poet' and will pay dividends when the children are ready to write down their first poems.

Take time to explore possibilities arising from a number of different pictures, always encouraging new ways of seeing.

WASHING MACHINE POEMS

Poems aren't all that difficult

Clothes whirled and twirled
like a merry-go-round, socks
and shorts, skirts and tops.

I stared into the eye of the
machine. 'The clothes look
like melted colour,' I said.

Mum was amazed. 'My boy,'
she said, 'You've made a poem!'
I didn't know it was so easy.

Moira Andrew

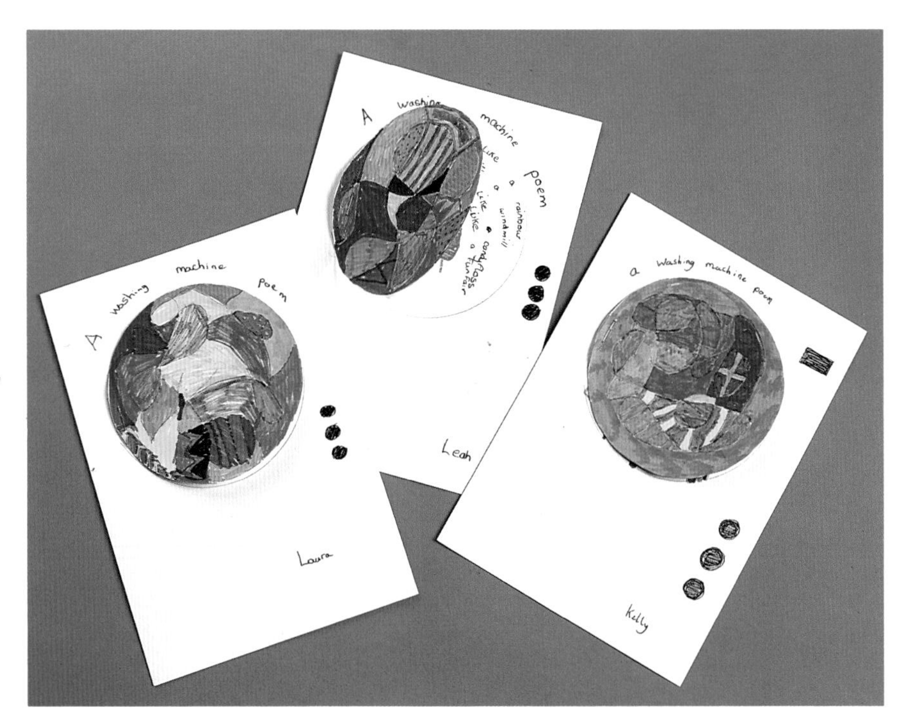

Read Moira Andrew's poem. Show an advertisement for a washing machine, and ask the children to think of more ideas for making a washing machine poem. They may suggest that the washing looks like spilled paint, a roundabout, party poppers, candyfloss.

For those children who are just beginning to write, make a one-poem book in the shape of a washing machine. The children can draw candyfloss, etc., on an opening circle. Inside they copy *'The washing looks like...'*, adding their own ideas to make an original image poem.

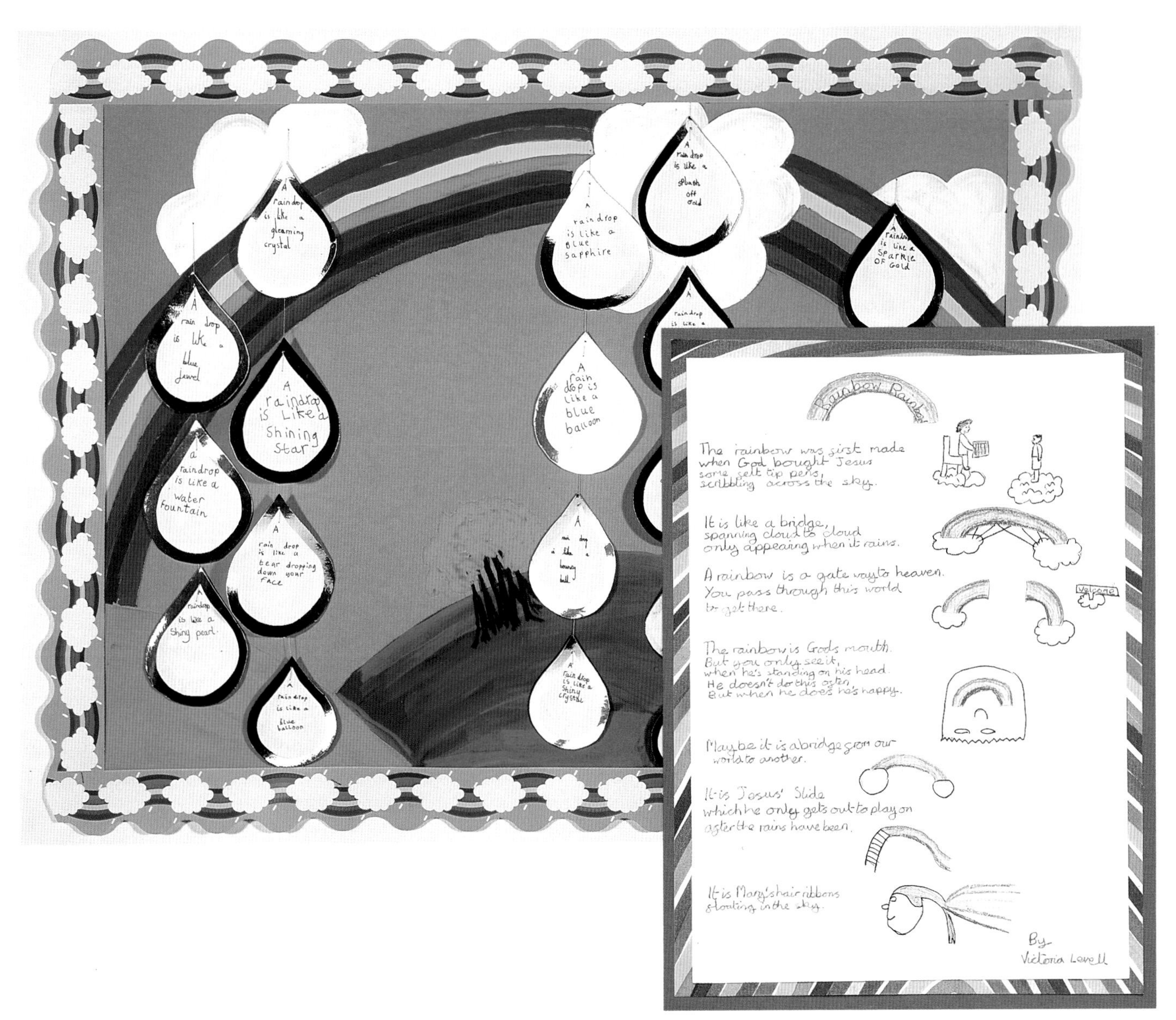

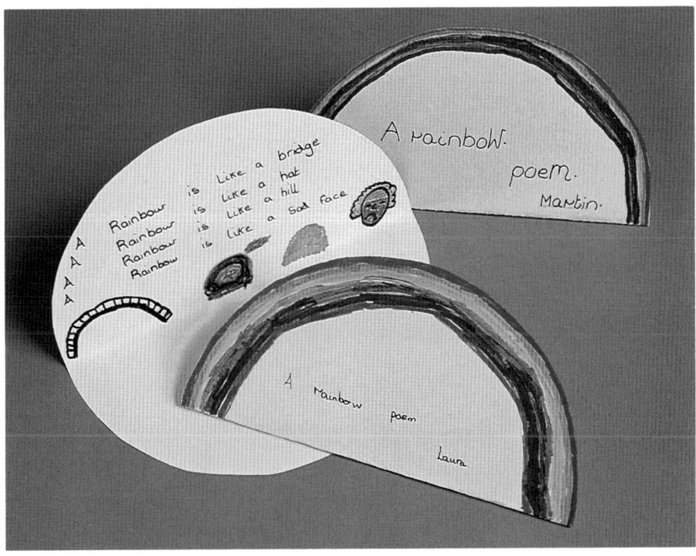

RAINBOWS

Using a picture of a rainbow and the 'magic hat' idea, collect a number of rainbow images orally. Make it into a game. For beginning writers, copy '*A rainbow is like....*', adding their own suggestions to make four-line poems. Using a teaplate as a template, make folded one-poem books as shown.

Make a rainbow display. On cut-out raindrop shapes, backed with silver card, the children should write one-line image poems (for example, either *A rainbow is like an umbrella* or, as above, *A raindrop is like a crystal bead)*.

Suspend the raindrops on cotton from a painted rainbow background. They will move and shimmer in the light. Add pictures and poems about rain and rainbows to complete the table display. Older children can develop the same theme, using quite sophisticated images. In the first verse of her poem, *Rainbow rainbow* , Victoria makes the connection between a rainbow and a packet of felt-tip pens! (See photograph above with the main display photograph.)

ON THE SKYLINE

For the youngest, pre-writing children, show a picture of sheep on a distant hill. Wearing their 'magic hats' the children will suggest that the sheep look like, for example, snowflakes, dandelion clocks, frost, white rose petals, etc. Read the poem 'On the skyline'. The poet suggested daisies for her image, but other ideas work just as well.

For children who are beginning to write for themselves, you might use a 'copycat' technique (see page 41). This allows the children to use a published poem as a pattern for one of their own, and ensures immediate success. To make this idea work, the children substitute their own images for those the poet has used.

Display the finished poems inside a frame of daisies, linked in a chain, or fold a circle in half to make a hill shape with white sheep glued, collage-style, all over it. Write the poem inside. ('On the skyline' also makes the point that poems don't have to be long!)

WEATHER POEMS

Weather makes an ideal starting point for poems, both for children who are just beginning to write, up to those at the top end of the school. Take advantage of the changing weather, so that the young writers have practice in the technique of using image, yet don't feel that they have done it all before!
For maximum success, encourage independent writers to copy the following simple poetry pattern using non-rhyming couplets. The first line should use an image, for example, *Rain is like a garden hose*, with a matching verb in the second line, *sprinkling the summer flowers*.

In the following photographs, the umbrella-shaped poem is by a seven-year-old, and the waterfall by a ten-year-old, using the same 'basic image' technique.

This method not only helps to make an effective poem, but encourages an in-depth exploration of language.

Snow

For major impact, you can't beat writing a winter poem to celebrate the first day of snow. Ask the children to sit silently as they watch the first flakes fall. Then group them in front of the board and ask them to think of images for the falling snow. To make it easy, suggest that they look first for something that you can cook with: for example, salt, flour, caster sugar.

Encourage the children to think of as many ideas as they can. Now write two of the ideas, shopping list style, on the board. Next look for flower images and, lastly, things that fly. Your 'shopping list' might look like this:

> ***SNOW***
> ***cooking ingredients:*** *salt, icing sugar*
> ***flowers:*** *dandelion seeds, almond blossom*
> ***things that fly:*** *dove's feathers, Cabbage White butterflies*

Suggest that the children use the 'borrow one, find one' technique (see page 4) to make their own shopping list. Each child can use an idea from the blackboard list, but must add a new one which has been thought up for themselves.

Once this is done - no emphasis on correct spelling at this stage - the children should then rough out their poems, perhaps using the pattern suggested above, for example:

> *Snow is like icing sugar*
> *sprinkled on a sponge cake.*
> *It is like sea-salt*
> *spilled on the kitchen floor.*

Encourage the children to look for a suitable verb to use at the beginning of each second line, for example: *sugar* can be *sifted* or *shaken*; *feathers* can *float* or *sail* or *fly*.

Display the finished work in a snowball shape using two matching circles, one to cover the poem, so that it is secret until the one-poem book is opened (see photographs above).

The Wind

Ask the children to suggest animals for their image of the wind: a bear, a lion, a wolf or an eagle will probably feature among their first ideas. Each of these gives a picture of a fierce stormy wind, so to encourage the children to explore language further, ask them to think of gentle images for a summer breeze: a fish, a butterfly, a swallow.

The youngest children can write simple one-liners, for example, *The wind is like a lion roaring.* These wind images can be copied individually on to strips of coloured paper and glued to the sails of a windmill or wind turbine picture.

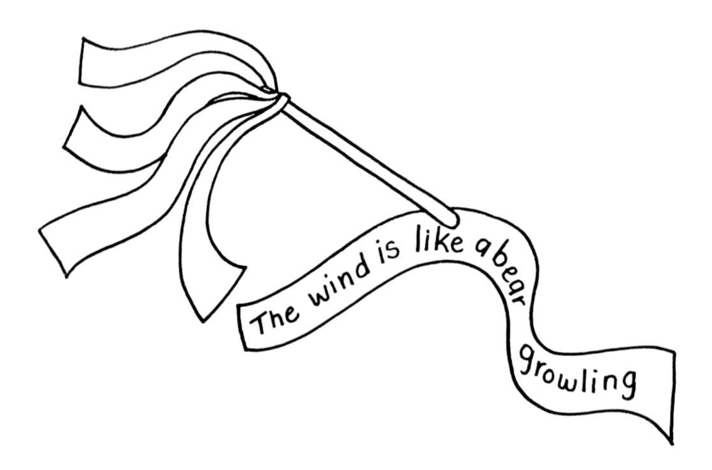

To make exciting wind poems for the children to run with in the playground, tape three or four images to a plant stick.

More experienced writers will think of and expand on a range of different images to describe the wind, as in the photograph below.

A poem by a ten-year-old begins with these delightful lines:

The wind is a wizard
enchanting the trees...

Suggest that the children work in pairs to find different ways of completing this poem, keeping a similar element of magic.

More weather poems can be started from images for frost, sunshine, thunder, lightning, fog, mist, and so on. Such poems can enhance science-based writing on a weather theme, bringing a different dimension to the children's work.

SUN, MOON AND STARS

The sun, moon and stars provide excellent starting points for poetry. To write a moon poem the children might look for toys *(a sailing boat, a boomerang),* foods *(a slice of melon, a pizza),* jewels *(a pearl, a wedding ring).*

Take some of the children's ideas to make a class shopping list. Then put together a group poem on the board. Let the children follow the 'borrow one, find one' rule to construct their own poems.
Despite similar starting points, no two poems will ever be quite the same! That is part of the magic of poetry.
As children grow in confidence, encourage them to seek out their own poetry patterns.
Emma has devised her own very effective 'without' refrain.

What is the moon?

The moon is a silver saucer without the cup.
It is a round tea-bag without the Tetley box.
The moon is an apple without the skin.
It is a Hob-nob without the crunch.
The moon is a ball without the bounce.
It is a buttercup without the pollen.
The moon is a peach without the juice.
It is a Rich Tea without the taste.
The moon is a sunflower without the seeds.
It is the world without the land.

Emma (7)

Read Emma's poem to the children and suggest that they write a similar poem following her *'without'* pattern - this time on the sea, mountains, the sun, space.

MACHINES

All kinds of machines make excellent starters for work in image - and the use of image, of course, gives life to poems on science themes such as transport, building a house, exploration of space, and so on. Encourage children to describe tractors as dragons, warriors or creatures from space; earth movers as prehistoric monsters or giants; aeroplanes and spaceships as birds, pterodactyls or ghosts.

THE ELEMENTS

Children can use their skill with image to write on fire, air, earth and water. **Let them use the non-rhyming couplet pattern, as Darren (8) has done for his poem on fire.**

Fire poems following Darren's pattern can be illustrated with fiery dragons or edged with flames. Use bright wax crayons, felt-tip pens or oil-based pastels.

POETRY SCULPTURES

Shaped outlines in card, or one-poem books, can add a display dimension to image poems - and most children enjoy the challenge of working in a new way. Sun, moon and stars have their own built-in shape! Moon poems can be displayed on shaped backgrounds of circles or crescents. Write sun poems out on a yellow circle, and star poems on star shapes.

For mountain poems, use a triangular background of purple or blue. Top with white for snow. The words of the poem can be written in a zigzag shape.

Display sea or waterfall poems on blue or green backgrounds cut to a wave shape, letting the words follow the curve. Add sequins to give sparkle to the finished piece.

For space poems, write in silver pen on black circles, perhaps putting the words into a spiral, and display among cut-out spaceships and space-walking astronauts.

Another way of displaying poetry sculptures is shown here. Print out the text on cloud/star/moon shapes and suspend as mobiles from wire coat hangers or crossed plant sticks.

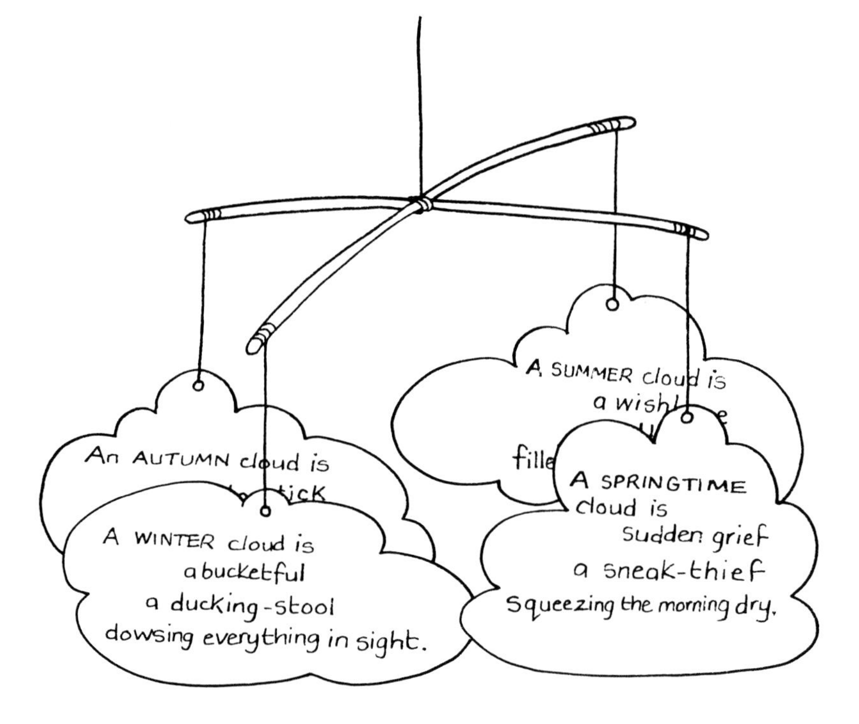

Flying high

To make an effective poetry mobile, write a series of poems on things that float, fly or belong to the sky: sun, moon, stars, clouds, hot-air balloons, birds, etc. Cut out poetry 'sculptures' that move in the air. Write poems on both sides of the sculptures, then hang them high on a string tied across the hall or classroom. It gives people the opportunity to read poetry from a new perspective.

EXTENDED IMAGE

When children move on to use extended image, they will work on a single idea throughout the poem. If, for example, they think of the sea as an orchestra, there will be a musical theme running through the piece.
If they imagine the moon as a face, they will write about its different moods and expressions.
Extended image is a useful technique for nine to eleven-year-olds to master, as it gives them a means of looking at quite ordinary things in a new and vivid way.
Read the poem Nicholas (10) has written about, of all unlikely things, a car showroom! He makes very effective use of one image from beginning to end.

A car showroom

Cars, like resting animals,
wait in the sun,
panthers ready to spring.
Outside more wait,
a pride of lions
at the drinking hole.

Shining glittering shapes,
the difference
visible only
to the discerning eye.
The garage sign
creaks in the wind
like a dead branch
high on the tallest tree.

THE SEA

If you visit the seaside with the children, encourage them to listen to the waves, to the wind, to water lapping on the beach. Ask them to think of musical instruments which make similar sounds. Note these ideas for later. Another method is to listen to taped sea sounds in the classroom. If this is to be a class poem, make a shopping list of ideas on the blackboard:

the wind - cello　　seabirds - flutes　　waves - cymbals, etc.

Encourage the children to think of a line with which to begin the poem, for example:

The sea is a band, or
The sea is like an orchestra

Then add two lines which connect the sounds of the sea with a different instrument. Perhaps it will look like this:

The sea is like an orchestra
where seabirds
scream like flutes
and waves
beat like drums.

Read Natalie's poem 'Orchestra of the sea' (see photograph). She has extended her image over four verses, always keeping music in mind.
Display the finished pieces inside a bubbling sea frame. To do this, write the poem in the middle of one sheet of A4 and cover it completely with another. Hold both papers up to a light or a sunny window and mark out the shape of the poem on the top sheet. Use pencil crayons or felt-tip pens to decorate the frame with sea creatures. Then cut out the marked-off hole and glue the frame over the poem.

Using the above structure as a basis, the children can follow it to write their own individual versions. Later they can be encouraged to use a different image as a starting point - the sea as an animal, a mythical creature, a garden, a magical world.

SOUND OF SILENCE

Ask the children to listen to quietness. Suggest that they think of four things they can do that make no sound, for example, listening, thinking, remembering, imagining.
Put some of these ideas into question form:

Can you hear me remembering
last year's summer holidays?
Does my brain make a sound
when I'm writing this poem?

Another way of tackling the poem is to think of four very quiet creatures (not a mouse, which is usually the first answer that comes to mind!). The children may think of spiders, butterflies, ladybirds, etc. Again encourage the children to turn their ideas into questions, for example:

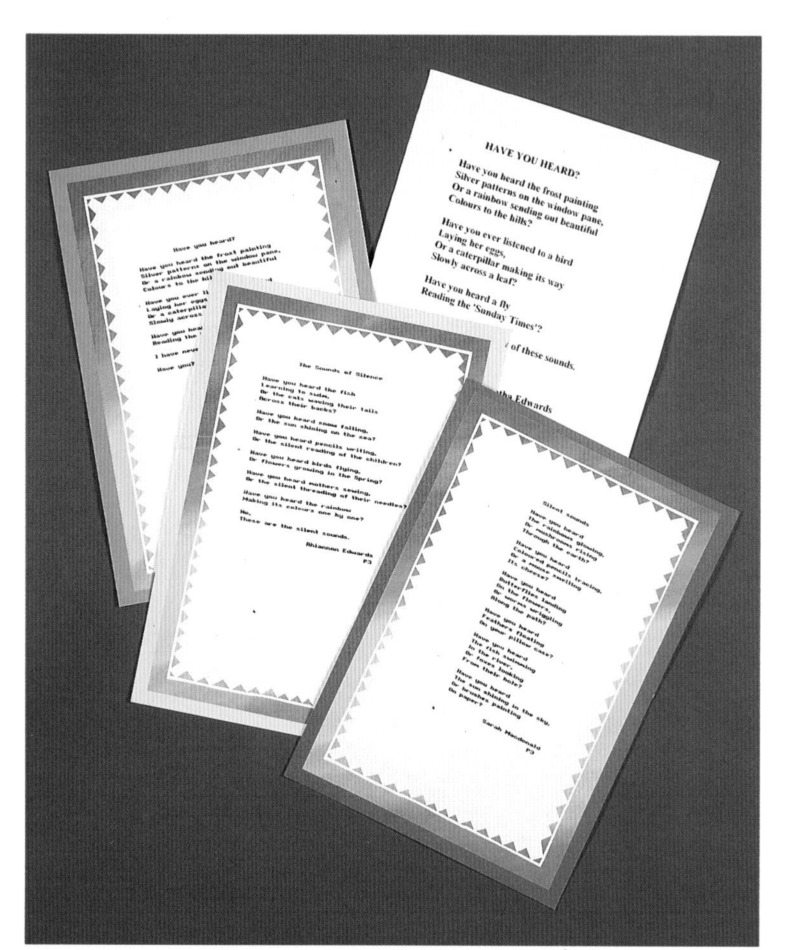

Can you hear a butterfly
floating on the breeze?
Can you hear a spider spinning
its silver web?

Older children should think of some unusual questions which make the ordinary world seem extraordinary:

Have you heard the grass
growing beneath our feet?
Can you hear a rainbow
being painted on the sky?

As suggested, the children can put their questions together to make up a poem, perhaps finishing it off with an answer.

No, these are the sounds of silence!

To write a similar poem called *Impossible sounds,* ask the children to work with a partner to think of some really zany ideas - a ladybird jogging, freckles growing on your sister's face, stars singing, the sound of the sun shining. Some of these ideas put together so that they have rhythm (not rhyme) can make a most unusual and exciting poem.

POEMS OF THE SKY

The sun, moon and stars carry their own magic image and can thrive in a poet's imagination. Suggest to the children that they take one idea about the moon - for example, looking like a face. They should think of a list of words and ideas connected with a face, for example, crying, smiling, shouting, staring.

The moon is a grumpy old man
snarling from the night sky.
He opens wide his silver mouth,
shouting instructions to the stars.

OR

The moon smiles from the dark,
caressing the stars in her arms.
She jokes with the clouds, singing
a lullaby to the sleepy world below.

Display moon faces showing the mood in the poems: laughing, crying, shouting, etc., glued collage-style on a night sky background, each with its own poem on a cloud-shape hanging underneath.

This photograph illustrates an effective way of displaying space poems. Show the writing on 'flying saucers' and surround with whirling space ships on a black and silver background.

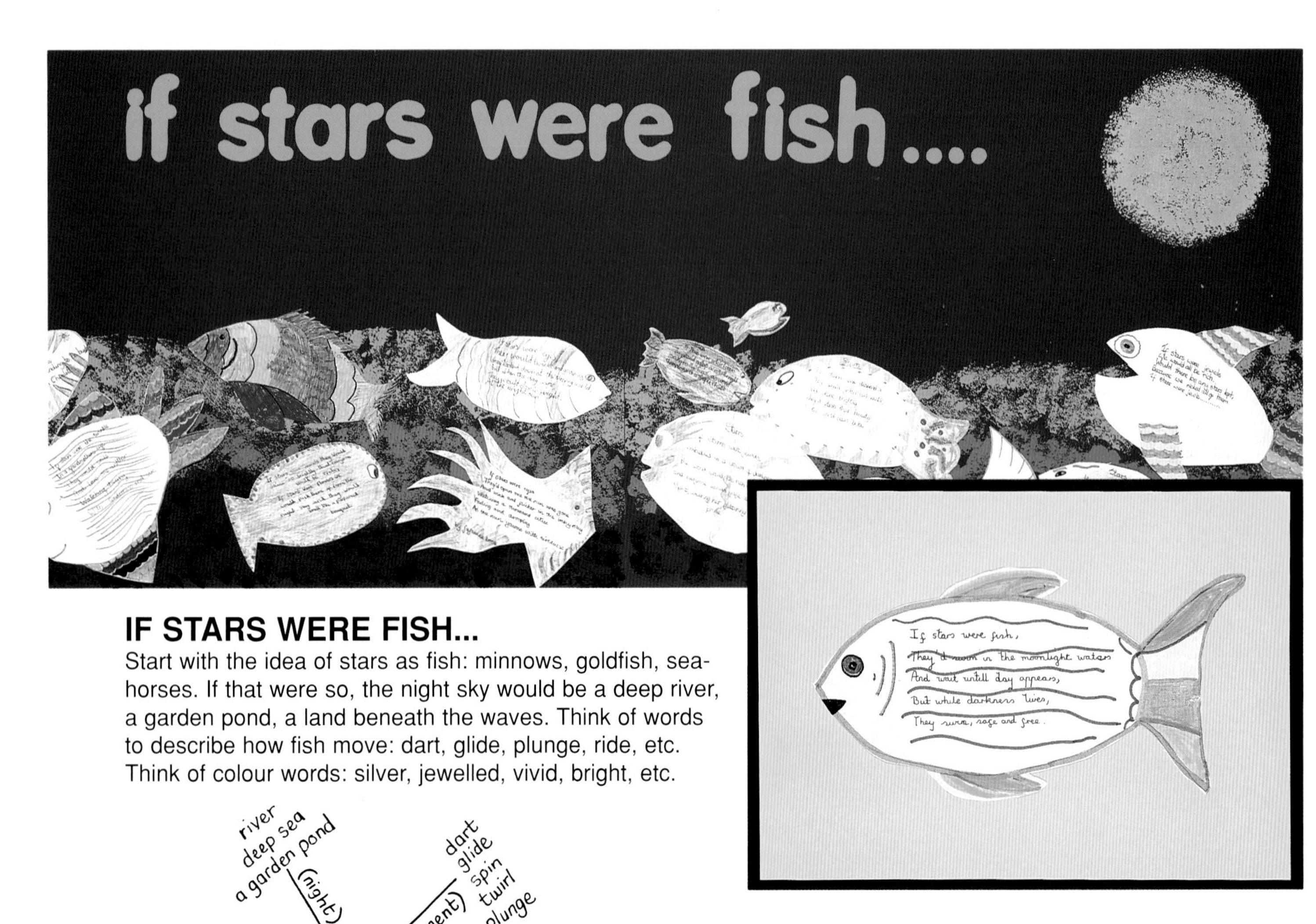

IF STARS WERE FISH...

Start with the idea of stars as fish: minnows, goldfish, sea-horses. If that were so, the night sky would be a deep river, a garden pond, a land beneath the waves. Think of words to describe how fish move: dart, glide, plunge, ride, etc. Think of colour words: silver, jewelled, vivid, bright, etc.

STARS
(night) river, deep sea, a garden pond
(movement) dart, glide, spin, twirl, plunge
(colour) silver, golden, jewelled, bright
(creatures) fish, minnows, goldfish, seahorses

Now put these words and ideas into a shopping list or topic web.

Put the ideas together to make a five-line poem. It might look something like this:

Night fishing

If stars were minnows,
they would flash across
the river of night, hiding
in its dark waters from
Fisherman-in-the-moon.

Moira Andrew

Suggest that the children use the topic web to make more extended image poems in a similar pattern.

If stars were goldfish/If stars were sea-horses...

Now try the idea of stars as flowers, of the sun as a balloon, of the moon as an eye, and so on. The list is endless!

Display: Write the star poems on fish shapes, cut out and pasted collage-style on a river/sea/underwater background **(see photograph above).**

LOOKING CLOSELY

It's all too easy to take the ordinary things of life for granted. Young children, however, have a freshness of outlook that allows unusual and exciting poems to spring from a creative exploration of the most mundane objects.
Let the children use their senses to handle, listen to, look at - even, as appropriate, to smell or taste - an everyday object such as a grapefruit, a shell, a buttercup, some pebbles. Encourage them to look with the eyes of an artist, explore with the zeal of a scientist, describe with the words and images of a poet. This way of working can make the ordinary extraordinary.

'EAT A POEM' TODAY

There are few edible poems, but this is one! Take in a shiny eating apple to school and let the children hold it, feel its roundness, turn it upside down. Let them smell the apple, feel the smoothness of its skin, shake it to hear if the pips rattle - sometimes you are lucky!
For the youngest children, those who are not yet ready to write, act as scribe (see page 4), writing on a clipboard a list of ideas: colour words, touch words, sounds. Hold the apple by its stem and ask what it looks like: *the rising sun, a Christmas tree bauble, traffic lights,* etc. Smell the apple. The children will say that it smells like *mown grass, cider, a fizzy sherbet sweet.*
Your clipboard will hold a mixture of words, phrases and images. Let the children help put everything in the best order. It may go something like this:

An apple poem

My apple is as red as the rising sun.
It feels smooth like my mum's skin.
It looks as bright as the traffic light
that tells us to stop. I can hear
the pips rattling about inside.
My apple smells of mown grass
and tastes like...

Now is the moment to cut the apple open, to look at the white flesh, at the pips inside. Make it a magic moment. Nobody has ever seen inside *this* apple before! Cut it into pieces and offer them round. Ask about the taste - *like a crunchy ice-cream.* Add the final line and remind the children that they have eaten a poem!
For those youngest children, make a wall poem in the shape of an apple. It is important that this is done as soon as possible, so that the children can 'read' it back. This activity helps to link reading and writing.

Six and seven-year-olds can write their own individual poems from the same starting point. Display them inside an opening 'apple' shape, so that the words are hidden until the title flap is opened.

Competent older writers can make secret poems. These should concentrate on the secret of new life hidden inside every apple, invisible until the apple is cut open. Like their younger brothers and sisters, they will enjoy the idea of eating a poem.

This kind of poem can be written about anything in the fruit basket. Because the apple is least messy, it is an excellent first choice, but let the children try *A grapefruit poem, A banana poem, A kiwi-fruit poem,* etc.

Display the finished work inside shaped opening poems and pile them together into a Harvest basket frieze.

SHELLS

A collection of shells makes a wonderful starter for writing at all levels in the primary school. Shells are readily available in seaside shops and come in a variety of interesting shapes and colours.

One way of starting out is first to hide a shell in a handkerchief. Let the children handle it and guess what is inside. Uncover the shell and talk about its colour and shape. Ask for suggestions for what it looks like and feels like. The extra bonus with many shells is that if the children listen they can hear the sound of the sea.

Again, for the non-writers, act as scribe, collecting words, phrases and ideas on a clipboard. Independent writers, in pairs or individually, can use a similar technique with a shell of their own choosing.

Here is six-year-old Phillip's poem about a cone-shaped shell. He has described it in minute detail, combining the skills of artist, poet and scientist.

My shell

As spiky as a pineapple,
Rough as a stone wall,
Bumpy like a road,
Pointed like a spike,
A cone spiralling upwards,
Stripy as toothpaste.
It is just like an
ice-cream cone
at the seaside.

Make a display of the shell poems on bands of wave-shaped papers: blues, greens and silver. To finish it off, add nets, a glass float, books about the sea and the shells, to a table display beneath the written work. **Give the children an opportunity to handle and write about other natural artefacts, for example, pebbles with an interesting shape and texture, driftwood, pine cones, coral or precious stones such as rose quartz and amethyst (as in the photographs at the top of the page).**

SNAPSHOTS

Use the 'looking closely' technique to encourage mini-poems and snapshots from garden, woodland or seaside 'finds'. Because these poems are short (five lines at the most), this method works well with reluctant writers.

Ask the children to look for a natural object which is small enough to be held in the hand: a fallen leaf, a daisy, a pebble, a crab shell, etc. Each child should have a plastic bag to store his finds, perhaps no more than five, all different. If you are on a woodland trail, suggest that the children only pick up things that are brown, so that they are not tempted to include wild flowers.

Back in the classroom, ask the children to look closely at their most interesting find. Let them handle it, shake it, turn it upside down, exploring shape and texture with eyes and fingers. On their shopping list, note colour words, how it feels and what it looks like.
Now put these ideas together in a five-line poem. Below are some snapshots by ten-year-olds inspired by winter garden finds.

Rotting stalk
Spiky as a hedgehog
Curved like a boat
Smelling of cucumber
A holly leaf

Ragged edges
Veined as wrists
Dark as plums
Little holes
A dead leaf

Old and musty
Brittle as bones
Crumbling and flaky
Dry as stones
A sliver of bark

It can look most effective if a number of snapshots are cut to shape and pasted on to a painted frieze of the winter garden.

The same snapshot technique works well when writing poems after a visit to a castle or a museum. This time the children will be unable to handle things, but they can look closely, noting words and ideas on their shopping list, before writing 'in best' back in the classroom.

The children might like to work in pairs, two concentrating on, for example, the arrow slits, others on the moat, the dungeon, the drawbridge, etc. Again, cut out and paste the poetry snapshots on the appropriate places on a wall frieze of the castle.

TREE POEMS

To many children trees are simply trees and they have not been encouraged to look at differences of shape or colour. They often find it exciting to learn tree recognition. Use a tree guide and start from trees in the school garden, in the park or on a woodland trail. Look closely at the leaves, the fruit, the shape of bare branches, etc. Think of colour and texture. Find ways of looking so that children think, in terms of image, what the tree looks like.

First look at the colour: *mint green, green as the deepest sea, ghostly green,* etc. Touch the bark. Is it smooth? knobbly? rough? What does the tree look like, for example, *an oak tree as wide as a river, a spruce as tall as a church spire, a weeping willow like a woman sobbing.*

For non-writers, use the 'teacher as scribe' technique from the children's dictation. For independent writers, suggest that they make lists of colour words, touch words, images, etc., putting their ideas together to paint a picture in the readers' imagination.

Below is an example of a group poem dictated by four-year-olds. The photograph shows a ten-year-old's close observation of a weeping willow.

Silver birch

The stem is smooth
like fur, and it's thin.
The leaves are arch-shape
and they are green and
yellow. Some of them
are falling off.

An excellent way of displaying tree poems is to make a frame of the tree outline **(as shown in the photographs above),** cutting it out and writing the poem inside the tree shape.

A number of tree poems of all different kinds, massed together, makes a very effective class or group display.

New Year's Day
MINISTRY OF FOOD
1953-1954
RATION BOOK

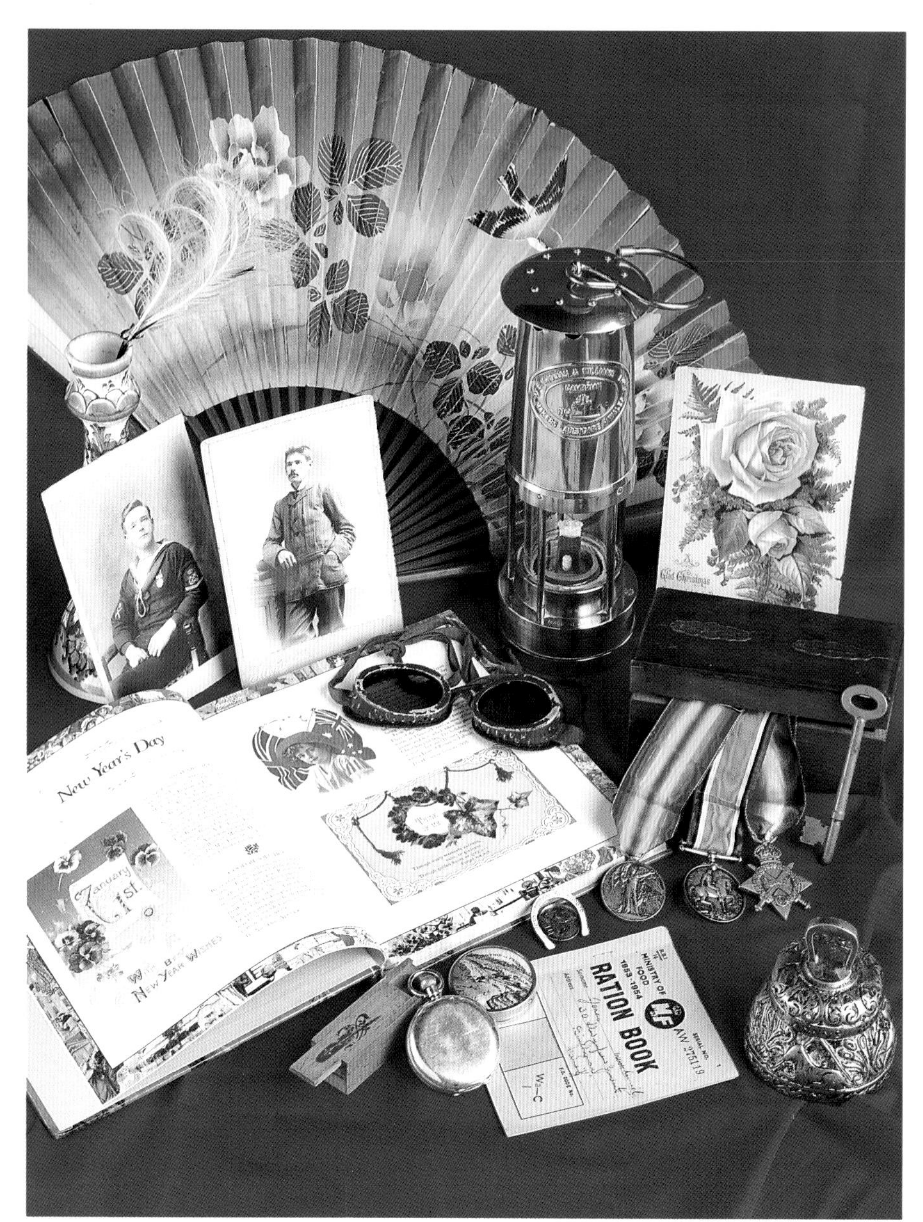

POEMS FROM HISTORY

With children of nine, ten and eleven, make a history corner, either collecting artefacts from one period, for example, the First or Second World War: ration books, identity cards, etc., or simply displaying a random selection of bits and pieces from junk shop or attic: a pocket watch, a fan, medals, boxes of all kinds, a gold ring.

First talk with the children, encouraging them to suggest what the various things might have been used for and who might have owned them. Build up mini-histories for each item. Let the children choose something that is of particular interest to them. Before they begin to write, the children should follow the 'looking closely' routine, thinking about colour, touch, sound, etc. Then they should move on to thinking about what the object is made from, what it was for, who might have used it, and so on. Encourage the children to combine direct observation with an imaginative leap, so that the resulting poem is both descriptive and personal.

Nine-year-old Claire writes about a First World War medal.

The soldier's medal

Delicate as a new-born baby,
sharp as holly hanging from your door,
shiny and still as water glinting in the sun,
beautiful as a butterfly flying past
is the medal of JA Jones.
He must have been proud to wear it
as bands played and old soldiers marched.

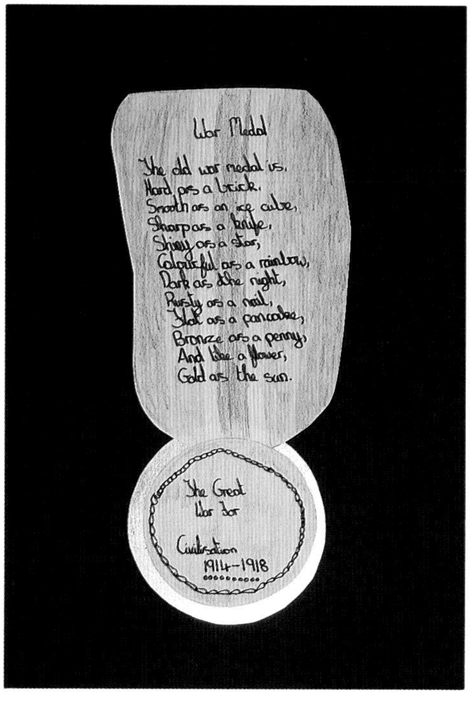

War Medal
The old war medal is,
Hard as a brick,
Smooth as an ice cube,
Sharp as a knife,
Shiny as a star,
Colourful as a rainbow,
Dark as the night,
Rusty as a nail,
Flat as a pancake,
Bronze as a penny,
And like a flower,
Gold as the sun.
The Great
War for
Civilisation
1914–1918

An effective and unusual way of displaying a First World War medal poem

NARRATIVE

The narrative poem comes from the ballad tradition. This does not mean that it must conform to the ballad form, but simply that it should be a poem that tells a story. Although it can rhyme, it does not have to, as its strength lies in the rhythm of the lines.

ONCE A SCARY THING HAPPENED TO ME

One way into the narrative poem with children in the 10-plus range, is to ask them to think of a time when they remember feeling very frightened. Think about getting lost in the supermarket, watching a scary video, being rushed to hospital, swimming too far out to sea, waking up in a strange place in the dark, and so on. Most children have stories of this kind to tell and are only too delighted to share them! Take time to listen and ask if they can remember how they felt at the time.

Suggest that the children blitz some of their ideas in rough, answering where? (setting the scene), who? (the people involved), how did they feel? (feelings, senses), what? (what was happening) and when? (time, season, age). They can also add scraps of conversation.

Then they must try to put it all together to make a coherent narrative - and this is where the skill of the teacher comes in. If children have difficulty in starting work on their rough outline, help them to tease out a first line which will capture the reader's attention. Go for something very direct:

'I simply couldn't believe it...',

'It was like this...',

One day when I was only two...',

'I remember once...',

'I had never told a lie...'.

Claire (10) has written a vivid account of a frightening experience remembered. Her low-key observation in the penultimate verse (answering what? and how?) brings the whole episode to life:

My gran couldn't do anything
but wring the hosepipe water
from her skirt.

Fire

I remember when I was six.
I was in my grans sitting room.
The fire was full of sticks.
'Click!' went my grans knitting needles.

Help! Fire! Help! Fire!
A shout through the wall.
My grandfather jumped up
And pulled my poor great-nan out.

Smoke billowed from the windows.
The Fire Brigade rushed up the drive,
And boy did they shout? They kept yelling
Is anybody hurt? Is anybody hurt?

My gran couldn't do anything
But wring the hosepipe water
From her skirt.

I sat down in the drive, silent,
And a tear or two streaked
Down my face.

Claire Kirby-Gould

FANTASY

Another way of introducing the narrative poem is to suggest that the children explore a childhood fantasy - again with attention to detail, feelings and scraps of conversation. Read *Summer to come,* by Rachel Hicks (10). Look at her skilful use of image, her apple tree *'like a little old man with a wrinkled smile'.*

Summer to come

The apple tree was old and small,
Like a little old man with a wrinkled smile.
The summer worn leaves hung ready to fall,
Waiting for Autumn winds to come.
One or two small apples lingered,
And a blue tit chirruped from branch to branch.
A worm eaten leaf fell,
And I crouched,
Still as a mouse,
On a branch of the 'Summer-to-come.'

"This" I said,
With a smile and a swing,
"This is the place where I will sing,
Where I will sing the songs of the sun,
The songs of picnics and summer fun."

'This' I said,
"Is the very place,
To build a house,
With a wooden base.
With wooden walls,
And a wooden roof,
All water tight,
And water proof!"

"This is the place,
Which in summers to come,
Will echo aloud,
With the songs of the sun."

Rachel Hicks

MEMORIES

All of us, children of primary age included, have a store of memories. These can be the trigger for a range of poetry - fun, lyrical, serious. Memory poems usually have a story to tell.

Suggest to the children that they (and you!) tell the story of *The first thing I remember: the funniest, most surprising, saddest thing that ever happened to me.* Make it a listening and story-telling session following the ancient oral tradition.

Before the children begin the task of writing their own story-poems, suggest that they brainstorm ideas connected with the colours, sounds and smells they associate with the incident. Get them to think too about the things people said. If the tale has become a family favourite, embroidered over time, ask them to consider why it sounds funny now, although it may well have been something of a tragedy at the time! Does time change our perceptions? These anecdotes are the raw material for the children's poems.

Choose three childhood memory poems from anthologies and read them aloud to the children as a 'starter' for their own written work.

Next give the children a set time (10-15 minutes) to write out their own memory experience in rough. This is called *'blitz writing'*. They can write in prose or poetry, using the style that comes most easily to them. At the end of the time limit, they must stop. This idea works best if the roughs are put away for a day or two before the children begin the task of editing.

When the children come back to their rough work, ask them to read it over carefully. Suggest that they cut out any words and phrases which slow down the narrative and make it 'story' rather than 'poem'. (A useful idea is to delete unnecessary *and's* and *or's*, substituting commas instead.) If the rough is still in prose, the children might need help to listen for the rhythms, so that the writing can be chopped into lines and finally into poetry format.

Richard's poem, *Visiting Nan*, has all the best elements of an early memory poem in which he has captured a wealth of fascinating detail - the cracked jar, the dusty smell, a well-remembered argument.

PORTRAITS

When children write portrait poems, they are painting pictures of people in words. They should choose someone they know well, so that they can highlight their mannerisms, what they look like and the kind of language they use.

Ask the children to sit silently for a minute or so to bring the person they have chosen into their imaginations. Ask some quiet questions to direct their thinking, for example, *What colour is his/her hair? Is it long, curly - doesn't he have much? What about the eyes? Think about the skin - smooth, prickly, tanned, wrinkled?* and so on.

Now suggest the children begin a shopping list or brainstorming which captures some of the characteristics of their 'sitter'; what they look like: *'thin as a stick', 'small and pretty like a flower', 'with a belly like a stuffed turkey'*, or a characteristic smell, *'peach blossom', 'cigarette smoke', 'aftershave', 'extra-strong mints'*. Think of height, build, way of moving, what they say, perhaps the kind of clothes they usually wear. This is like an artist's outline.

From their shopping list, the children should choose an opening line which is very direct, encouraging readers to read on. It should be so individual that it paints a portrait of *their* Grandma, Grandad, mother, uncle, etc., and no other person in the world!

Below are some opening lines that ten-year-olds have used for portrait poems:

The smell of peach blossom...

Huge gold-framed spectacles...

White hair, clear blue eyes...

Grandad was old, about 89
with patches of thin white hair...

My mum has short curly hair.
She wears long flowing skirts
and light brown tights...

She has white hair
and is still very pretty
After 90 years of wear
and tear...

My auntie is as thin as a stick,
she smells of sweet perfume...

My dad is a silent man,
can't stand people telling him
what to do.
He's all for the quiet life, is dad.

Many of these led on to describe where they lived or something that happened. Others remained simply portraits, poems in their own right.

Grandad

Grandad was old, about 89,
with patches of thin white hair.
I remember that to the end,
he would smoke all day long,
puffing out great clouds of smoke.

He would always sit
in his favourite chair
reading and coughing away.
He used to blow up balloons
then let them go flying
around the room.

Then, like the air in the balloons
disappearing,
so did the life in my grandad.

Tim Stean

These two portrait poems are in very different styles, but each paints an individual and compelling portrait.

Ha Ha Ha Ha

Mr Pollard

Before he went to Spain,
Our teacher,
Mr. P.
Or Pollard,
Wore bowties
And laughed
a lot.

He still laughs all the time
Our teacher,
Mr. P.
Or Pollard,
Now he doesn't wear bowties
Anymore,
It's too hot.

Vicki Hunter

Display the completed poems in pen-and-ink frames as an 'art gallery in words'. You might like to paste a photograph of the sitter behind his/her portrait, asking viewers first to guess the identity of the sitters, before checking with the photograph. This can sometimes lead to sadness, sometimes to hilarity - especially on parents' evenings!

My mum...my dad

The youngest children can also write portrait poems. As with their older brothers and sisters, they should begin with people they know well - mum, dad, grandma and so on.

Suggest that they use a simple formula:

My dad is..........and................
He looks like a ....
Sometimes he says.................
And..

This will result in poems like those shown below:

My dad is big and strong,
He looks like Fireman Sam.
Sometimes he says, 'Enough is enough!'
And then you know he's not joking!

My mum is small and pretty.
She looks like a fluffy hen.
Sometimes she says, 'Well, just this once!'
And I give her a big kiss.

Such a formula will enable the children to get words down on paper, but encourage those who want to experiment to move on from it, suggesting that they try out new and different ideas of their own.

This is another successful formula, one which encourages young children to think in terms of simple image.

As...............as a ....
as.................as a ....
as.................as a ....
She's................just like....

My Teacher

As pretty as a peacock,
as bossy as a bee,
as clever as a calculator.
She's magic, just like me.

If...

Another way of tackling portraits (and for this idea I am indebted to Sandy Brownjohn) is to suggest that children imagine what their 'sitter' might be if they were a fruit, a bird, a vehicle, a colour, an animal, etc. This becomes the first two lines of the poem. Then they have to think about why they have chosen that particular description - shape, colour, movement, and so on - indicating why in subsequent lines. This idea gives another imaginative dimension to the portrait poem.

If my favourite auntie was a pot of paint
she'd be sky-blue
colouring the paths of life.
If my favourite auntie was a boat
she'd be a ....

If my uncle was a bird,
he'd be an old pelican
with well-worn feathers,
all grey and white.
If he were a tree,
he'd be a...........

If my grandma was an animal
she'd be a fluffy white Persian
rubbing against the hearts of people
and making friends everywhere.
If she was a fruit,
she'd be a ....

If my mum was a drink
she'd be a glass of cool fresh water
like a bubbling brook,
a running laughing stream.
If she was a biscuit,
she'd be a ....

CONVERSATIONS

Conversation poems give the children a great deal of scope. Good dialogue is one of the most effective ways of giving a poem life, and children are totally familiar with the phrases that adults use - and often over-use - as far as they are concerned. Let them collect some of the sayings of mum and dad, teacher and dinner lady. Having identified such choice phrases as *'Right now!' 'Time for bed/trumpet practice/homework!' 'Now I'm telling you for the last time!' 'This is for your own good...'* and, of course, all the *'Don'ts - 'Don't let me see you chewing with your mouth full!' 'Don't use felt-tips in the bedroom!' 'Don't get your new sweatshirt dirty!' 'Don't run in the corridor!' 'Don't slam the door!'*

Ask the children to make up a *'Don't!'* list poem. Many of the children feel that this is something of a subversive activity and thoroughly enjoy working on it.

Another way of writing a *'Don't'* poem is to list six *don't* ideas, changing the word at the end of each to give the poem a surreal flavour.

Don't put mustard on ....the school gate.
Don't climb up ....a rainbow.
Don't slam the ....
Don't lose your ....
Don't write on ....
says our teacher, but we don't listen!

Try question and answer poems - the zanier the better.

How far is it to the moon and back?
As far as the bike shed on a wet Monday afternoon.

What is the best way to write a poem?
Dip your pen in silver paint and wait for the sun to shine.

If you met a Stegosaurus what would you do?
Jump on a magic carpet and fly to the moon.

How would you paint the stars?
Climb the highest mountain and perch on the tallest ladder.

CHOPPED-UP POEMS

Take a published four-line poem or write four lines on the seasons.

In springtime daffodils bloom in the dark earth.
In summertime sunshine sparkles like diamonds on the sea.
In the autumn leaves are painted red and yellow.
In wintertime snow turns the garden white.

Now mix up the lines to make new and surprising poems.

In springtime daffodils sparkle like diamonds.
In summertime sunshine blooms in the gardens.
In the autumn leaves fall like paint on the dark earth.
In wintertime the sea is like a snow-white garden.

Try a simple senses poem, then chop it up so that the senses are mixed up. Then extend each idea into a second line.

I like the taste of toothpaste.
I like the smell of roses.
I like the feel of sunshine.
I like the sound of church bells.
I like the look of mountains.

I like the sound of mountains
clinking against the sky.
I like the taste of sunshine
tingling across my skin.
I like the feel of roses
stroking the summer sun.
I like the smell of church bells
fragrant in the winter air.
I like the look of toothpaste
squeezing wave-tops on to the sea.

Children can have a great deal of fun with this kind of poem and are often very excited by the result.

USING A FORMAT

Children - and adult! - writers often respond to working to a structure. A structure provides both security and a challenge. If formats are varied and interesting, the resulting poems will reflect this variety and the children will feel that they are tackling a new and different task each time.

Children need to grow as writers, and teachers need to be able to monitor this growth. Within the guidelines of a structure, able children should be able to stretch their writing imaginations while less confident souls will feel a certain safety knowing that they are not being asked to write poems in a vacuum.

Most children, asked to write a poem on 'spring' without some kind of starter structure, will be totally at a loss and many will experience a sense of panic. 'What do you want me to do?' and 'Where do I start' they ask! For those children, the provision of a format makes the impossible possible. (See *Recipe for spring*, page 37.)

LISTS

A red poem

The list poem is the easiest structure of all. Children who are beginning to write can copy a phrase such as *Red is ....*, adding their own word and picture. Suggest that they should write at least four lines and, hey presto, a poem!

It is often best first to sit in the book corner with a group of children. Talk about things that are *always* red: *strawberry, post box, cherry, lipstick.* On a board, use some of the children's words to make a list poem, showing how each new idea goes on a new line. The first poem might look like this:

> *Red*
>
> *Red is a strawberry.*
> *Red is a tomato.*
> *Red is the post box.*
> *Red is my mum's lipstick.*

The children who have their own ideas will soon extend this list poem, often unexpectedly adding feelings, for example: *Red is when I feel angry. Red is my face when I can't stop laughing.*

For six and seven-year-olds, move on to other colours, suggesting a green poem, a yellow poem, and so on. A gold list is an excellent idea for a Christmas poem.

Display the children's work above a red/green/blue table holding books, paint pots, drapes and artefacts in the appropriate colour.

Another method of colour poem display is to cut three circles from sugar paper or coloured card. Use the primary colours, red, blue and yellow. Using a saucer as a template, cut a hole near the edge of each circle and back with tissue paper in a matching colour.

Write a blue poem on the blue circle, yellow on the yellow, and red on red. Then overlap the tissue circles on the classroom window, as shown. The overlapping red and blue tissue will look purple, the red and yellow appear as orange, and the yellow and blue will show as green. This makes an unusual display, combining simple poetry-writing with some understanding of colour mixing.

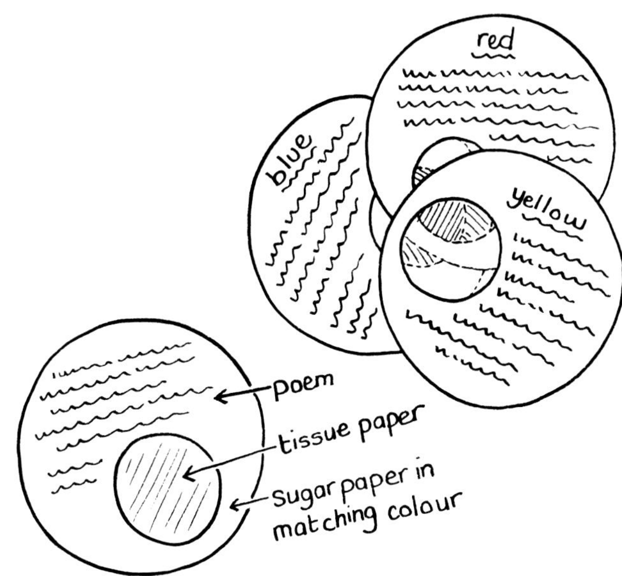

If the children have shown an interest in linking emotion to colour, ask them to suggest an angry colour, a sad colour, a lonely colour and a happy colour. The poem develops ideas they may have used in their first colour list poems.

To display the feelings poem, use a four-page zigzag format, writing a verse on each page. Colour the page lightly in pencil crayon, edging each verse with waves, buttercups, poppies, etc., as appropriate. A contoured top to each page, jagged for anger, downturned for sad, a smooth curve for lonely, and so on, gives the zigzag book an extra dimension.

In five minutes

Another effective list poem can start from thinking about time. Using a stopwatch, gather the children together and ask them for ideas about what you can do in a second, one minute, five minutes, and so on.

List the answers and write them out in the form of a poem.

In one second

I can
clap my hands,
blink a bit,
smile at my baby brother.

I can
stamp my foot,
poke out my tongue,
shout at my little sister.

I can
say I'm sorry,
dry my eyes,
give my mum a big kiss.

On the move

This list poem works well with a transport topic, especially if the children have been involved in doing a traffic survey. They should first make a note of all the different vehicles going past the school gate, for example, cars, lorries, a bus, a tractor, etc. Think about the sound each makes. Talk about ways of starting their lines. Some children might opt for *Here comes, Up goes, Look out for,* etc. A poem may take the following format.

On the move

Up go the cars. Zoom, zoom
Up go the lorries. Brmm, brmm
Up goes the school bus. Grrh, grrh
Up goes the farmer's tractor. Chug, chug
DOWN come the cars. Zoom, zoom
DOWN come the lorries. Brmm, brmm
DOWN comes the school bus. Grrh, grrh
DOWN comes the farmer's tractor. Chug, chug

CRRRRRRRRRRRRRRASH!

Five, six and seven-year-olds love making all the traffic noises. Display all the finished poems on a sloping frieze, as though they were going up and downhill.

Celebrations

Celebrations of all kinds offer an opportunity for an interesting list poem with six and seven-year-old writers - especially useful for giving an unusual slant to Christmas. Talk with the children about what a celebration means, what different kinds of celebrations they can think of: Christmas, birthdays, Diwali, etc.
Ask how we celebrate, how we feel, what we see around us, etc. Again, for beginning writers, offer a simple way in, such as: *Celebrations are ....* Suggest that the children work on at least six lines.

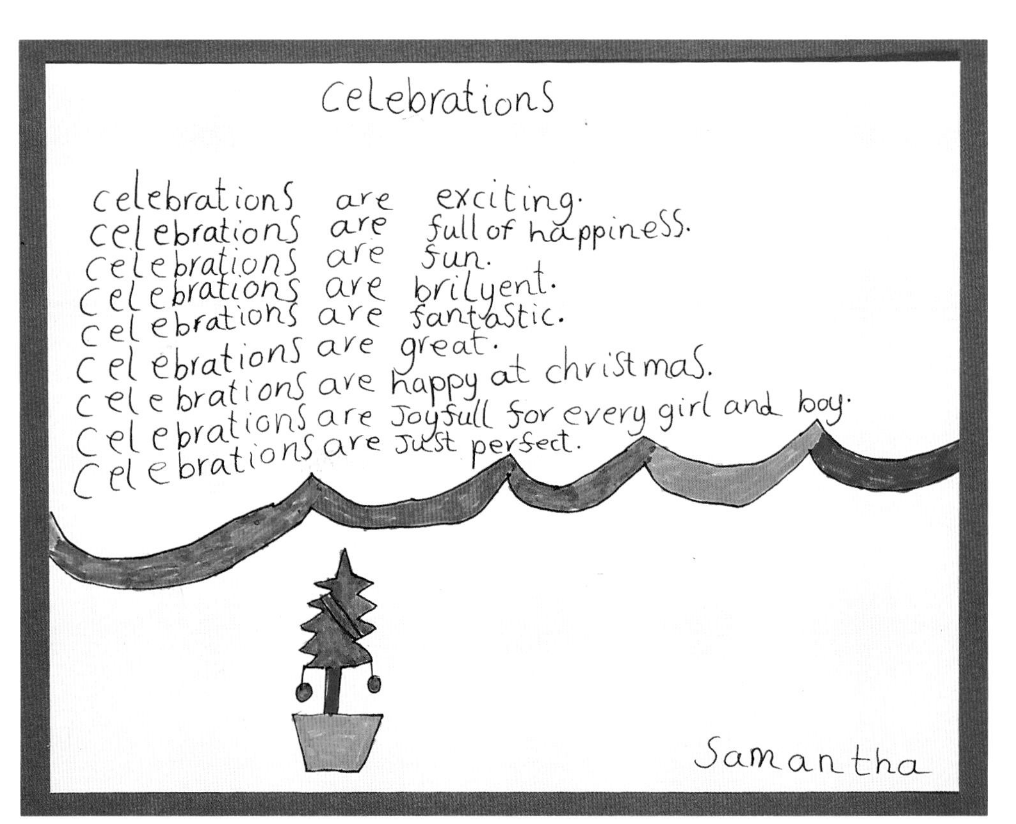

Samantha (6) wrote this poem at Christmas.

Remembering

List poems can still work well as children move up the school. Lee (8) did not find writing easy. When his Grandma died, he wrote this touching poem, based on the simple list format.

The remembering

I've remembered to take flowers.
I've remembered to put them in a pot.
I've remembered where the grave is.
I've remembered to pray because I loved Nan
and also I've remembered to cry.

Suggest other simple things to remember, for example, holidays, each line using a different sense: I remember how cold the waves felt/ I remember how fishy the harbour smelled/ I remember how bright the sun looked/ I remember how good the ice-cream tasted/ I remember how loud the seagulls screamed/ I remember a fantastic holiday!

The haunted house

Children at the top end of the primary school can enjoy writing frightening poems. Suggest that they think of the various rooms in a haunted house: the cellar, kitchen, hall, dungeon, bedroom, attic, etc. Get them to list the rooms on one side of a folded A4. Opposite, they should list four things that might be found in each.

For example, *In the cellar - a tin trunk, a wrinkled hosepipe, a rusted bicycle, a dusty sack.* They should now expand each idea until it reads: *a tin trunk full of cobwebs, a wrinkled hosepipe full of holes, a rusted bicycle with no wheels, a dusty sack full of bones.* Now they should think of a spooky sound to go with each room in the haunted house.

The haunted house

In the cellar is
a tin trunk full of cobwebs
a wrinkled hosepipe full of holes
a rusted bicycle with no wheels
a dusty sack full of bones
and the only sound
is the eerie song of the wind.

In the attic is
a rocking chair running with mice
a broken doll with only one leg
a box full of faded photographs
a vase filled with long-dead leaves
and the only sound
is a rumble of distant thunder.

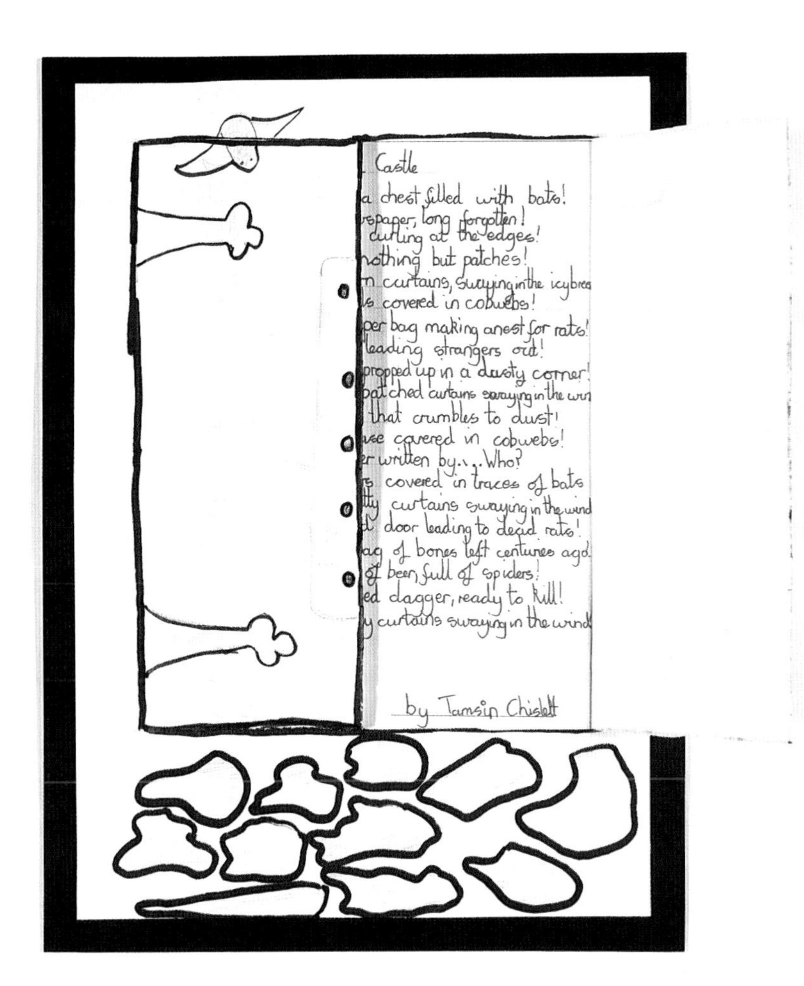

The children should follow the same pattern, listing four ghostly things to be found in each room, followed by the line *and the only sound is ....* with a different spooky idea each time.

Display the finished piece on a haunted house shape with a heavy door opening to reveal the poem. The children can make use of dark paper and silver pens to great effect. Add spiders, ghosts and bats, etc., collage-style.

SEQUENCES
Through the year

This is a simple format for a poem, based on either seasons or the months of the year. For the youngest children, think of an apple tree in each season. It can take this form:

The apple tree

In springtime,
look at the blossom.
In summer,
look at the leaves.
In autumn,
look at the apples.
In winter,
look at the bare branches.

There are a number of ways of displaying *Through the year* poems. **For the youngest children a four-page zigzag works well (see photograph above).**

This sequence format allows the more able writers to write more sophisticated poems, still sure in the knowledge that it must fit into a simple four-verse pattern.

Try sequence poems based on clothes we wear (hats work particularly well), games we play, the garden/park/seashore through the seasons.

Days of the week and months of the year can be tackled in a similar way.

Older children can use an A4 sheet divided into quarters, with a verse in each. *The tree seasons* poems were written and illustrated by nine and ten-year-olds.

Another interesting method of display uses the 'stage-set', which depends on folding and cutting A4 paper, as shown. This makes a four-sided freestanding 'book', ideal for showing a four-verse poem to advantage.

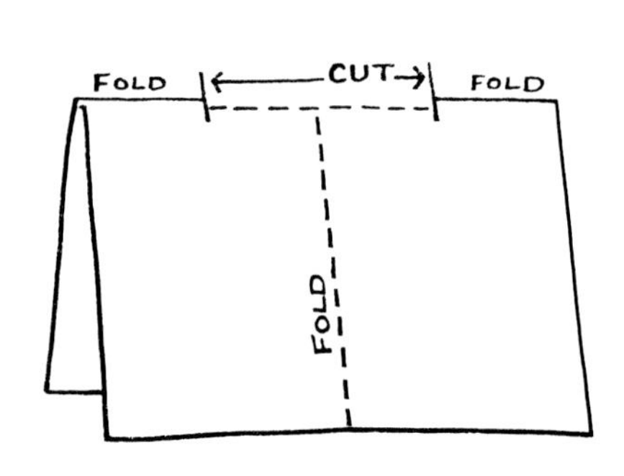

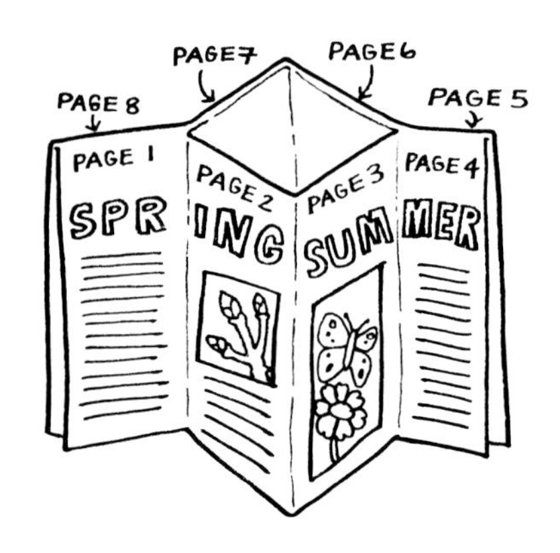

The butterfly's story

The story of the butterfly, the frog, the dragonfly, the toad, etc., can fit neatly into a sequence poem. For the youngest children, use a four-page zigzag with simple text. For example:

The butterfly's story

Look at the egg lying,
lying on the leaf.
Look at the caterpillar crawling,
crawling on the flower.
Look at the chrysalis hanging,
hanging on the fence.
Look at the butterfly flying,
flying in the air.

Children's choice

Once established writers understand the concept of sequence poems, their own ideas are often very imaginative.

For example, *A water sequence,* from a raindrop to the ocean; *Growing old,* a birth to death poem; *The poem I'm writing,* a sequence from the tree in the forest to the paper on which the poet is writing his poem!

Debra (10) wrote 'The chessmen', a most unusual sequence poem.

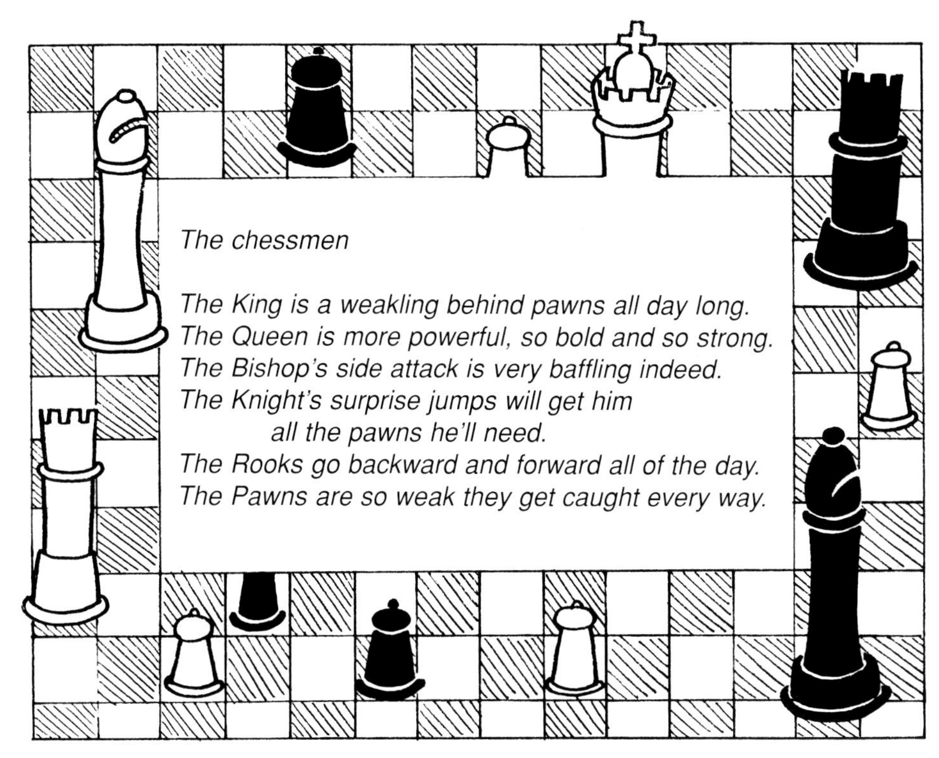

RECIPE POEMS

Recipe for a dragon

Look first at a selection of recipe books with the children. Look for the words used to direct the cooks: *Take, mix, add, stir, whisk,* etc. Talk about what a recipe is used for, how one first collects all the ingredients together, how the recipe is followed until the mixture is ready to be placed in the oven, and so on.
Suggest that we are going to write a recipe poem, showing how to make a dragon. As nobody has ever seen a dragon, we can use our imaginations to create something quite out of the ordinary. A good way into this piece of work is to ask the children to write down all the different parts of a dragon in a long list - head, back, spikes, scales, wings, tail, teeth, eyes, claws - and, most important, breath.
Now suggest to the children that they look for the roundest brightest thing they can think of to make the dragon's head - *sun, moon, hot-air balloon.*
The children should write their own idea in its place on their shopping list. It may read:
head - moon *body - Mars* *spikes - pyramids,*
and so on.

On the board, show the children how to put the poem together. In the first verse, collect the 'ingredients', beginning with *Take* (3 lines). Now use *Add* or *Mix* to make a second three-line verse. Then, perhaps, *Decorate with* to introduce the third verse. Finally, we must *Stir in* the dragon's breath and bake the whole thing for a very long time.
The poem may look something like this:

Recipe for a dragon

Take a *head as bright as the moon,*
a body as red as Mars
and spikes pointed like the pyramids.

Add *scales overlapping like an eagle's feathers,*
wings as green as the ocean
and a tail winding like a river.

Decorate *with eyes shining like stars,*
teeth as cold as icicles
and claws as dangerous as daggers.

Stir in *breath as fiery as a volcano.*
Put in a very hot oven
and bake for a hundred years -
and you have made a DRAGON!

BEWARE!

Follow a similar format to write *Recipe for a mermaid, a unicorn, a Phoenix, a Cyclops, King Neptune,* and so on. To make this kind of poem work, the children must be encouraged to let their imaginations soar. They should use this format to describe mythical creatures, not real animals.
When this poem is finished, the children can make very successful one-poem books from two sheets of A4 stapled at the side. The poems should be divided into six parts, each inside page showing writing at the top, illustrations beneath. The outside cover should be decorated and show title and author.

On the last page, the children can make a pocket to hold a mini-book: *The dragon's photograph album, The Dragon's diary* - even *The Dragon's Filo-fax!*
Display the books on a background of collage-style fire and flames in red, yellow, orange and silver paper.

Follow the recipe format to write *Recipe for spring, summer, autumn, winter* poems (see photograph).

TURNABOUT POEMS

This format requires a certain sophistication in the writers, and works best with children of ten and eleven.

First make a mini-thesaurus of words connected with a volcano or a river, using the board. (Verbs are particularly useful.) You might have two separate lists like this:

volcano	***river***
red	*flow*
fiery	*meander*
erupt	*fish*
smoke	*gush*
burn	*current*
blaze	*whirlpool*
dangerous	*swirl*
frazzle	*splash*
scorch	*flood*

Now tell the children that they are not going to write about either a volcano or a river. This is a turnabout poem, so they have to write, for example, about The school, A motorway, or The supermarket, using as many volcano words or river words as they can. This helps children to write some vivid poems, often enabling them to use strong verbs.

Christopher (10) used river words to great effect in his motorway poem. The second poem by Rachel (11) owes much of its immediacy to the language collected for a volcano.

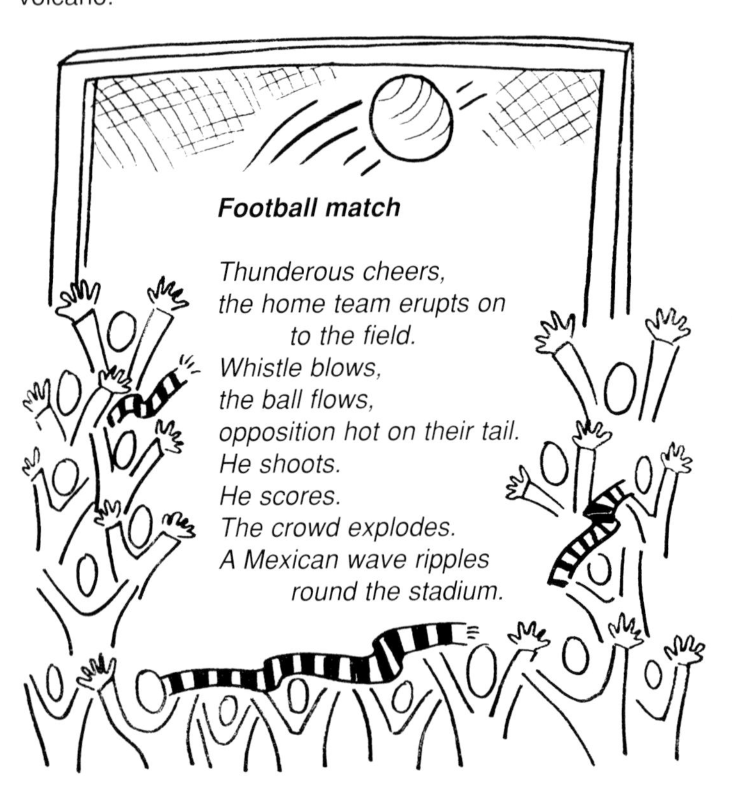

Football match

Thunderous cheers,
the home team erupts on
to the field.
Whistle blows,
the ball flows,
opposition hot on their tail.
He shoots.
He scores.
The crowd explodes.
A Mexican wave ripples
round the stadium.

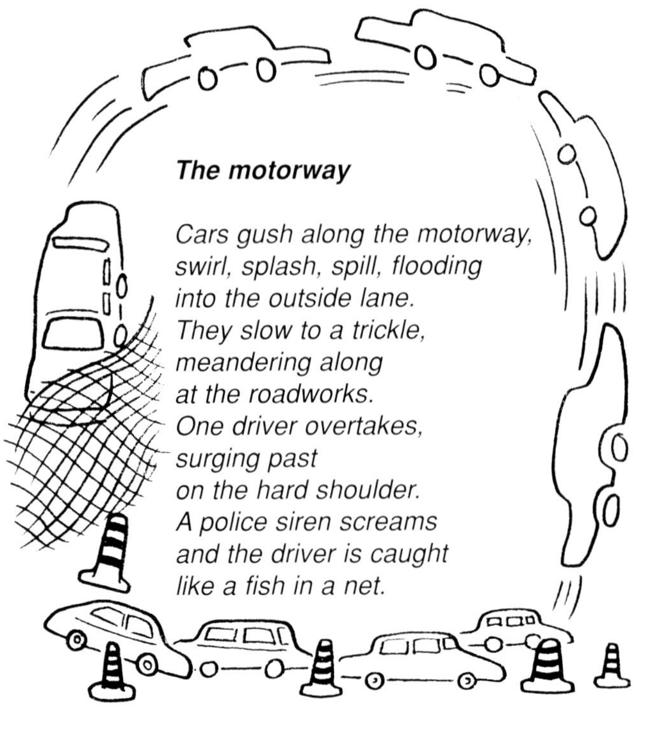

The motorway

Cars gush along the motorway,
swirl, splash, spill, flooding
into the outside lane.
They slow to a trickle,
meandering along
at the roadworks.
One driver overtakes,
surging past
on the hard shoulder.
A police siren screams
and the driver is caught
like a fish in a net.

HAIKU

The haiku is a traditional Japanese poem, short and formal. In its English version it has 5-7-5 syllables, usually in three lines. It works best if it has one main image - every word should count. As the poet James Kirkup says, 'The qualities of haiku are brevity....and surprise.' At its best, the haiku should make us look again at an everyday event and open our eyes with shock.

Despite its brevity, the haiku is anything but an easy option. However, many children have such a freshness of outlook, that they can use the strict form to paint vivid word pictures. They usually enjoy syllable-counting and regard the haiku as an intriguing puzzle to be solved!

To give practice in syllable-counting, suggest that the children start with their own names, breaking into groups depending on the number of syllables in their first names. Make up a rhythmic piece, clapping to each beat in their names. Move on to flower names, animals, place names, etc.

To begin working on haiku, suggest that children make up some five-syllable lines that might make an interesting way into a haiku. Try *On a mountain top, On a winter's day, In the morning sun, In the heat of day, On a London bus, Down our busy street,* etc. Let the children choose a line from the flipchart or board to work on. It can be made into a group competition, each using a common first line, but aiming to get that element of surprise or contrast essential to the haiku.

In the morning sun
all the doors stand open wide
and secrets spill out.

In the morning sun
washing hangs limp as dead birds
and bright flowers fade.

In the morning sun
children run barefoot and free
but grown-ups can't cope.

Working on the puzzles set by haiku helps children to reconsider and reorganize their poems, not settling for the first ideas that come to mind. It gives them a reason to search for alternative words, and to rehearse synonyms.

Ask the children to look around the playground or the school garden to target some ordinary things as a subject for haiku, remembering always to focus their 'poet's eye' so that they can make an acute observation.

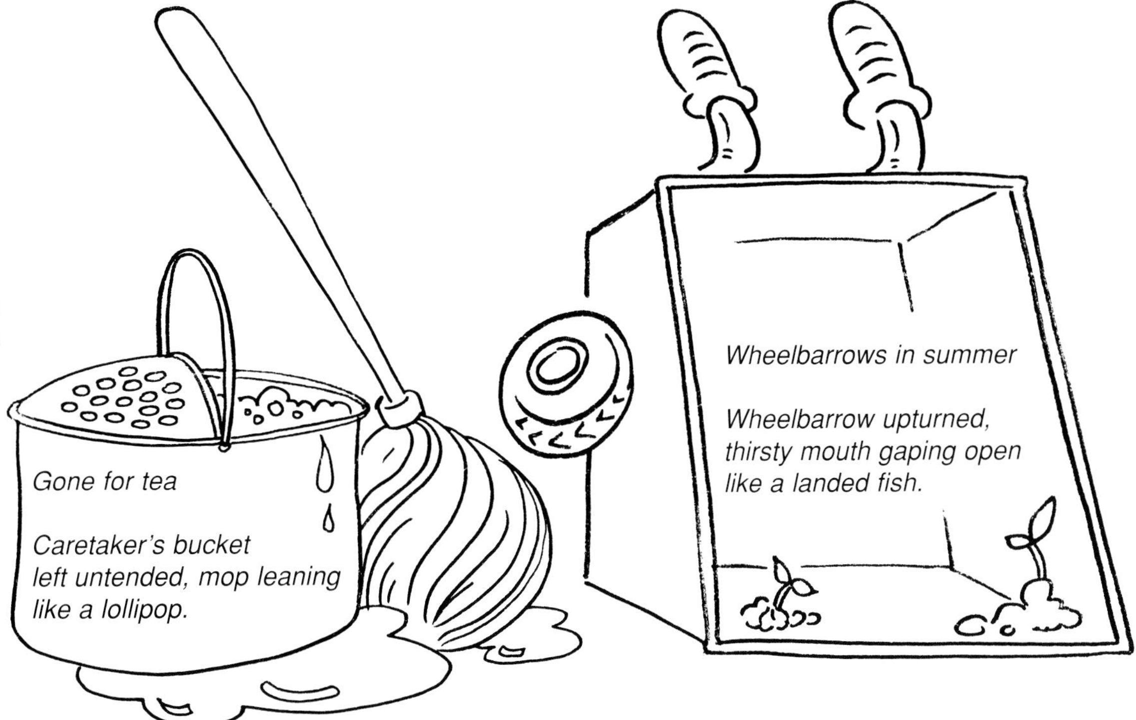

CINQUAIN

The cinquain is another form of syllabic poem. It is of five lines with 2-4-6-8-2 syllables in each, so it is more complicated than the haiku, but offers a similar challenge. Again, the ability to use an arresting image gives the cinquain its sparkle.

Autumn, (2)
black birds flutter, (4)
alight on high-stretched wires, (6)
like notes for an overture to (8)
winter. (2)

ACROSTIC

The acrostic poem can be read downwards as well as across, the initial letters making up the title of the poem. The strict discipline of this form makes a puzzle which children often enjoy solving. Use the acrostic form to encourage the less confident children to 'have a go'. They can write about themselves, using the letters of their name, trying to describe things they enjoy doing, things they detest, characteristics, how they look, and so on.
The acrostic is useful for seasonal poems and poems about each month of the year. Think of CHRISTMAS, for example. On the board, collect ideas for each letter. (For the initial C: children, church, candles, carols, Christchild; H: holly, home, happiness, hymn.) Help the children to collect and expand these ideas about Christmas. The very youngest can make a simple list poem.

C*arols*
H*olly*
R*eindeer*
I*vy*
S*tockings*
T*rees*
M*ince pies*
A *baby*
S*tars......*
CHRISTMAS!

More established writers will be expected to expand these ideas to make each line describe something more about Christmas, perhaps thinking about how it feels and what it means to us.

Carols ringing loud and clear,
Holly wreaths on every door,
Reindeer galloping across the skies,
Ivy gathered from the woods.
Stockings hung on ends of beds,
Trees in windows shining bright,
Mince pies baking in the oven.
A special baby lying in a manger,
Stars guiding Kings across the sand .....
..... That's CHRISTMAS!

If children want to experiment with rhyme, the acrostic is ideal. It can be quite humorous, allowing inversions and half-rhymes.

Carol-singing in the frosty air
Holly wreaths all down the stair.
Reindeer galloping across the night
Ivy looped with tinsel bright.
Stockings hanging on ends of beds
Trees decorated in golds and reds.
Mince pies ready, spicy and hot
A baby in a manger cot.
Stars to guide kings all the way.....
.....And we wake up to Christmas Day!
(Group poem)

Display Christmas acrostics in star-shaped outlines on a dark background which shows the manger scene in silhouette.

Acrostics, with their long, often narrow shape, are ideal poems to turn into bookmarks. Use these as small gifts on Mother's Day, Valentine's Day, etc. Make bookmark acrostic poems to celebrate Book Week, special outings to the museum or library, or in honour of a member of staff who is leaving.

COPYCATS

It is generally accepted that we have no need to reinvent the wheel. Likewise, we can encourage children to use some of the patterns and structures developed by poets over the years. Far from inhibiting creativity, this method often releases language and ideas in those who need a helping hand with poetry-writing. It takes away some of their perceived difficulties and solves the business of where to start.

New nursery rhymes

Nursery rhymes give a range of starter patterns. Suggest that the children change them a bit at a time - names, for example:

Mary had a little lamb can become *Harry had a little hen* or *Sarah had a mischievous mouse....*

Harry had a little hen
with feathers gold and red.
She loved to be with Harry,
so she followed him up to bed.

Harry had a little hen
with feathers red and gold.
She laid him eggs for breakfast
and did as she was told.

This kind of poem must rhyme, of course, and should follow the original rhythm, but it need not make complete sense.

Sarah had a mischievous mouse,
whose whiskers were all tickly.
He chased Sarah with a holly leaf
till she went quite pink and prickly.

Sarah had a mischievous mouse,
whose whiskers were all tickly.
He tickled her nose, he tickled her knees
and she ran away quite quickly.

Look at nursery rhyme books, suggesting ways of changing the first line, perhaps bringing it up to date.

For example: *Sing a song of twenty pence* or *Sing a song of sailors, spacemen, sausages.* The following lines should in some way match the ideas in the first.

Sing a song of twenty pence,
a pocket full of sweets,
four and fifty tummy aches
after all those special treats.

Sing a song of sausages,
sizzling in the pan,
four and twenty Boy Scouts
waiting with a Billy-can.

Have fun with *Humpty Dumpy sat on a stone/fence/floor,* or *Daniel McSpaniel slid on the ice; Dr. Foster went to Bath/in a shower of sparks; Little Miss Muffet sat on a tuffet, eating her chips and egg, pie and beans...* and so on.

New nursery rhymes can sometimes be used to good effect to make a social comment.

There was an old woman
who lived in a box.
She had so few possessions
she'd no need for locks.
They gave her some soup
with two slices of bread,
Then she wrapped up in rags,
made the pavement her bed.

Moira Andrew

A week of weather

Read Wes Magee's poem, 'Week of Winter Weather'. It is another list poem, describing the weather on each day of one week. This poem rhymes, but the copycat doesn't have to.

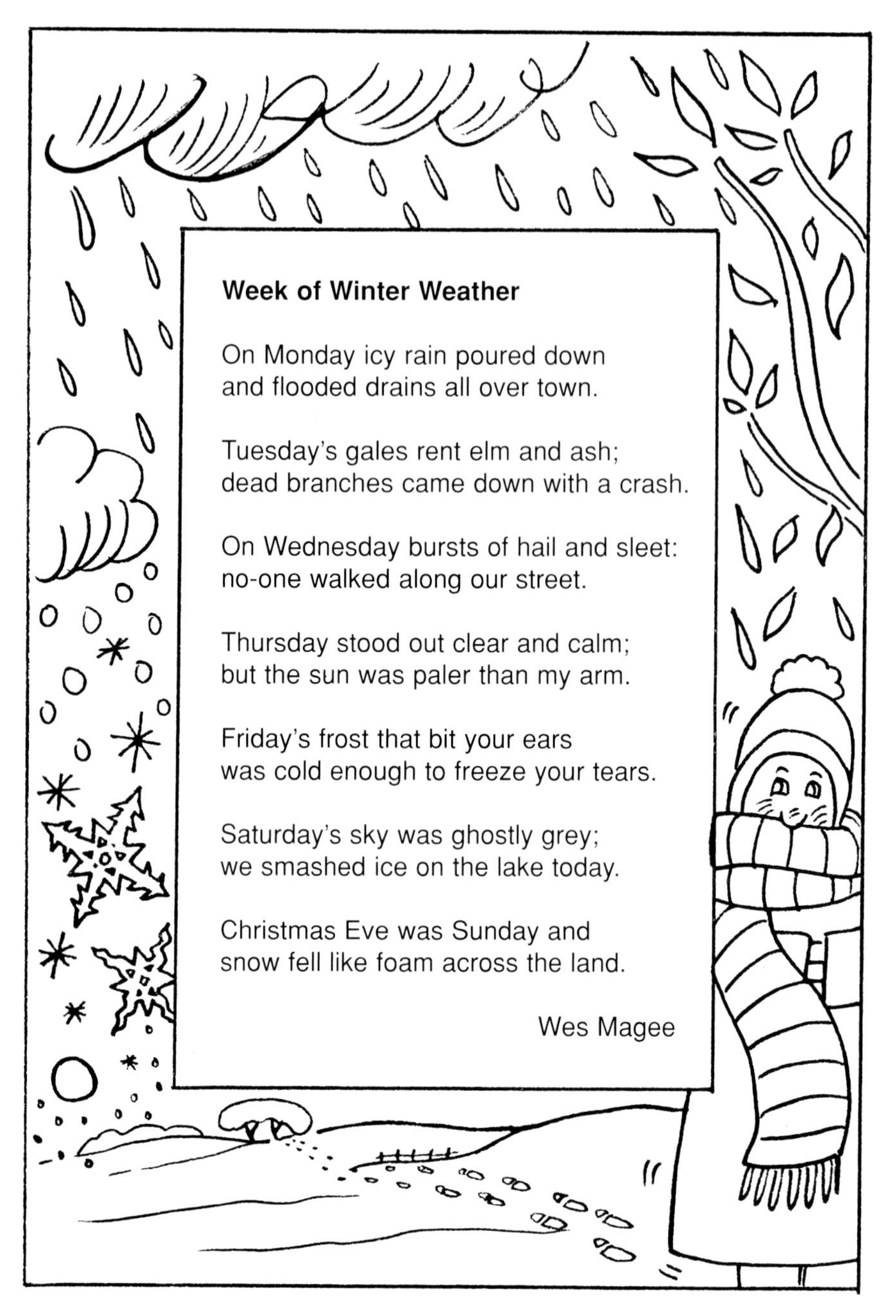

Week of Winter Weather

On Monday icy rain poured down
and flooded drains all over town.

Tuesday's gales rent elm and ash;
dead branches came down with a crash.

On Wednesday bursts of hail and sleet:
no-one walked along our street.

Thursday stood out clear and calm;
but the sun was paler than my arm.

Friday's frost that bit your ears
was cold enough to freeze your tears.

Saturday's sky was ghostly grey;
we smashed ice on the lake today.

Christmas Eve was Sunday and
snow fell like foam across the land.

Wes Magee

Young children can write a copycat poem to this pattern. Keep a weather watch for a week. Sometimes it doesn't vary from day to day, so they can invent different weathers for themselves.That's what being a poet is about - a poet has the power to change things!

A week of springtime weather

On Monday it was wet and windy
and daffodils bent their yellow heads.

On Tuesday clouds flew across the sky
and shadows danced in the garden.

On Wednesday the sun shone like gold
and..................

and so on.

The children should use their weather watch list to write their first lines. The second line of each couplet should introduce something about springtime which the children can observe, either from a nature walk or from the classroom window.

LETTERS

Dear Weather

When children write letter poems, they can use their new-found writing skills in an exciting and imaginative way. Suggest to the youngest children that they write a letter poem to the weather. Imagine asking for snow at Christmas, for sunshine on your birthday, for rain when you have shiny new boots!
To begin a Dear Snow poem with the youngest children, ask them to suggest colours and feelings about the snow. Think about clothes to wear and things to do. Put some of the words in list form on the board. It might look like this:

snow - cold, white, fun, sparkly
woolly hat, boots, gloves
snowballs, sledging, snowmen

Help the children to put their ideas into the lines of a poem, asking them to suggest when they would most enjoy having a fall of snow, what they would wear and do, and so on. Either make it into a group piece, acting as scribe, or get beginning writers to work on a line at a time, using words and ideas from the board. Below is a group poem, written by five-year-olds.

Dear Snow,
Please come to my Christmas party.
I'll wear my woolly hat and my boots.
You are so cold and white and sparkly
I think you are a lot of fun.
I'll sledge down the hills.
I'll make snowballs to throw.
I'll build a snowman in the garden.
Please come to my Christmas party.
Love from ....
(Each child adds his/her name.)

Emma (6) writes a poem to the rain. (It owes much to her experience of writing list poems.)

Dear Rain,
I want to splash in the puddles,
Jump in the puddles,
Paddle in the puddles
In my shiny red boots.
Please rain soon.
Love from Emma

Dinaspowys Infants
Cardiff Road
Dinas pawys

Dear Rain
I want to splash in the puddles.
Jump in the puddles
paddle in the puddles.
in my shiny red boots.
plese rain soon.
Love from Emma.

Display the letters (with envelopes and hand-designed stamps) on a red and yellow background, like The Royal Mail, placed above a table display of books related to the mail service, the postman, letters and cards. Edge with a border of used stamps or of the children's own designs.

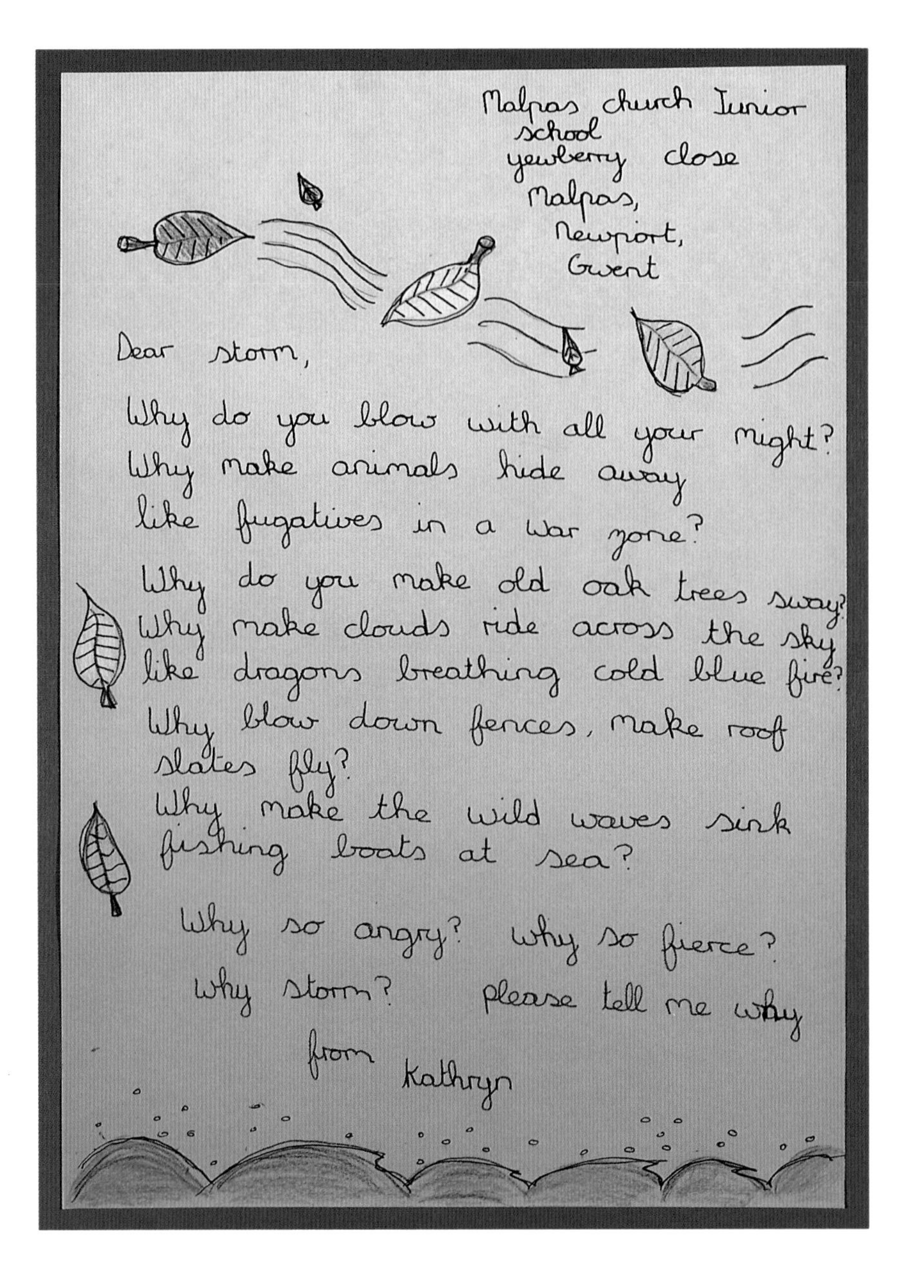

Malpas church Junior
school
yewberry close
Malpas,
Newport,
Gwent

Dear storm,

Why do you blow with all your might?
Why make animals hide away
like fugatives in a war zone?
Why do you make old oak trees sway?
Why make clouds ride across the sky
like dragons breathing cold blue fire?
Why blow down fences, make roof
slates fly?
Why make the wild waves sink
fishing boats at sea?

Why so angry? why so fierce?
why storm? please tell me why

from Kathryn

More experienced writers will enjoy tackling a different form of letter-poems written to the weather (see photograph above). They should think of weather which threatens us in some way - blizzards and storms, perhaps. Discuss the damage that severe weather can cause. Make a shopping list of weather words, linking sounds with musical instruments, as in the poem below. The poems can be written as a series of questions addressed to the weather:

Dear Wind,

Why do you scare us in the night,
rattle doors like castanets,
roll dustbins around like drums,
shake blinds like crazy tambourines?
Why don't you let us sleep
wrapped in safe summer dreams?
Why? Please tell us why.

From Year 5B

Dear Storm,

Why blow down ancient trees
with your strong cold breath?
Why whistle through broken branches
with your spooky woodwind voice?
Why whip up white-topped waves
with your angry winter song?
Why are you so spiteful
huffing and puffing at the world?

From Alison

Display storm/wind/blizzard poems on paper cut to a spiky outline, edged in silver and glued into place over a forest scene in silhouette, or a stormy sea in dark blues and greens with tossing ships shown in silhouette.

Letters from history

Experienced writers can write letter poems either to or from an historical character. This kind of work can be linked with a history project, as some background knowledge gives the poems a certain veracity. Thinking themselves into a character also helps children to understand more about how people from times past actually felt.
Once they have chosen the character and the situation, the children should think about how these people might have felt - lonely *(Scott of the Antarctic),* frightened *(a passenger on the Titanic),* excited, *(WW2 pilot searching the skies),* etc. The children might begin by making notes about their feelings, thinking of why the letters were written, what people wore, and so on.

Read *Letter from Egypt* by Moira Andrew. Here the poet tries to think herself into Mary's head as she writes to thank her friends for putting her up at the inn.

Letter from Egypt

Dear Miriam,
Just a line
to let you know how things
are with us & of course to
thank you (& your good man)
for all you did for us - &
at your busiest time too
what with the census &
everything. I was quite
exhausted & the baby was
beginning to make himself
felt. If it hadn't been
for your help that night
my baby might have died.

Good of you
to put up with all our
visitors - who'd have
thought, six scruffy
shepherds up & leaving
their sheep like that?
& didn't they ever smell?
Still they were good-
hearted & they meant well.
I hope they brought some
extra trade to the inn.
They looked in need of
a hot drink & a meal.

& what about
those Kings, Miriam? Kneeling
there in their rich robes
& all? & me in nothing but
my old blue dress! Joseph
said not to worry, it was
Jesus they'd come to see.
Real gentlemen *they* were.
But what funny things to
give a baby - gold & myrrh
& frankincense. That's men
all over! It wouldn't cross
their minds to bring a shawl!

Sorry we left
so suddenly. No time for
good-byes with King Herod on
the warpath! We had to take
the long way home & I'm so
tired of looking at sand!
Joseph has picked up a few jobs
mending this & that so
we're managing quite well.
Jesus grows bonnier every
day & thrives on this way
of life, but I can't wait
to see Nazareth again.

Love to all
at the inn.

Mary

Moira Andrew

Just for fun

Write some unusual letter poems just for fun. Try to make these poems rhyme. Try *Dear Mr. Noah, Dear King Neptune, Dear Doctor Dolittle, Dear Mrs Pepperpot,* and so on, taking ideas and characters from stories, poems and mythology. Try *Letter to a unicorn, Letter to a Hobbit,* or *Letter to a wizard.*

INVITATIONS

Poetry can be involved in other different forms of writing, such as invitations. These can work equally well for real events or for purely imaginary ones. Try invitations to the harvest supper, the Christmas play, the end-of-term concert; or suggest that children invite a Martian to tea, or imagine themselves as woodland animals inviting their friends to a late-night party in the forest, or as chessboard pieces inviting *The Borrowers* (Mary Norton) to a picnic.

Dear Grandma,
Please come to school on Friday night.
If you're here at seven, you'll be just right.
It's our harvest supper with bread and cheese,
And tea and cakes, there's lots of these!
And music and dancing and songs to sing,
And our prayers of thanks for everything!
Love from Sarah

Dear Marty Martian,
Beam on down to
36 Ashgrove Road
on July 26, 07.45,
(our planet, our time).
Chill out with us
Earthlings over a
wild chilli burger
and a red root beer.
Yours terrestially, Nick

Make your real invitations as informative as you can. For the fantasy invitations, let your imagination go into overdrive!

WORD HEAP

Collect a set of words (nouns, verbs and adjectives) at the level for which you intend the children to write. You might ask children to suggest words about the sea. Gather a set of sound/touch/colour words, etc. Write these ideas on the board.

sea	*waves*	*green*	*breaking*
	seagulls	*white*	*screaming*
	boats	*red*	*rocking*

From the board, show beginning writers how they can use the words to make the bones of a poem. Make it into a poetry game, adding more words as necessary, but attempting to include all those listed. For example:

Postcard from Cornwall,

Green waves breaking,
red boats rocking,
white seagulls screaming,
golden sun shining.

The sea in winter

Deep green waves,
breaking white
against the rocks.
Red-painted boats
rocking, cradled
by harbour walls.
Black-headed
seagulls screaming
into the wild wind.

Write the word heap sea poems on to cut-out boat shapes and paste these on to a sea background (as in the photograph).

Another way of building a word heap, with more advanced writers, is to take a selection from a well-known poem. (Those below come from the third verse of 'Fern Hill', by Dylan Thomas.)

sun	*fields*	*playing*	*owls*	*long*
high	*lovely*	*sleep*	*grass*	*fire*
green	*stars*	*hay*	*running*	*flying*
moon	*flashing*	*chimneys*	*horses*	*dark*

From the words in the heap, the children should try to build up a picture, first in the imagination, then on paper. They should use as many of the above words as they can, adding others such as *it, was, all, to, the, into, and,* etc.

When the children have finished, read the Dylan Thomas verse and compare it with their newly-written poems. This exercise helps to make the point that no two poems ever turn out the same - even where they use common words and a similar starting point. Discuss differences of emphasis, content and style.

Display the completed poems on a 'hills and fields' background alongside the original. Use a computer print-out for the 'Fern Hill' verse.

SHAPE

Children much enjoy the challenge of shape poems. They can vary from simple one word shapes to quite complicated poems which both follow the shape and express the action of the subject of the poem. Shape poems make excellent classroom displays.

Climb every mountain

Ask the children to think about mountain-climbing. What might they see/hear/feel at the top of a tall mountain How would they get there? What special gear would they need?

Make lists of words and ideas on the board. Find a starter phrase for the youngest children, for example, *On the mountain top...........* Follow this with: *I/we see..............., I/we hear.........., I/we feel..............,* etc. A simple poem might look like this:

On the mountain top,
we see clouds
we hear the wind
we feel very cold.
It is a long way d
o
w
n

or

On the mountain top
clouds sail like boats,
winds howl like ghosts,
it is cold as winter.
We daren't look d
o
w
n

On the mountain tops see clouds hear winds feel cold It's a long way d o w n

Decoded, this poems reads: *on the mountain tops, see clouds, hear winds, feel cold.* It uses many of the ideas first offered by the children. They enjoy this way of working enormously. Even those who profess to hate poetry find pleasure in solving the shape puzzle.

Snakes, caterpillars, hosepipes, mountains, roads, waves, etc., make starters for linear shape poems with the youngest children. As above, collect words and phrases ('six things you know about caterpillars') then fit them into an appropriate shape.

Fireworks and fairgrounds

Fireworks, roundabouts, helter skelters, the Ferris wheel and switchback rides make interesting shape poems for more sophisticated writers. They should again think of colour, sound, movement words. In the Catherine wheel poem below, Stephen (8) thought of *fizzle, crackle, pop, red, blue, green, turquoise, golden, whizzing, round and round, showers, sparks, stars, spinning, shooting.* Give children a specific target, for example, 'ten describing words to go with rockets'.

Stephen first wrote,

Fizzle, crackle, pop
round and round
a shower of stars
red, green, turquoise
and blue, golden rain
shooting spinning flashing
whizzing sparks zipping
into the darkest night.

Then he designed his firework shape poem with eight segments and filled in the spaces so that each line had its own space.

Claire has illustrated her sparkler poem in a similar way (see photograph).

Make a firework, rocket and bonfire frieze for Bonfire Night. Use silver, gold, red, orange and yellow foil paper cut into flames. Add Guy Fawkes and people around the bonfire in silhouette. Cut out the firework shape poems and paste into place.

Weather shapes

Use rain, clouds and lightning as starters for shape poems.

Lightning
zigzags
across
the sky
like
bright
yellow
ribbons
flying high

ONE-WORD POEMS

This is another starter which needs quite a bit of ingenuity on the part of the children, but one which they much enjoy. Look for letters which have their own meaning, for example, B, C, G, I, O, P, Q, T, etc. Think of B hive, C U tomorrow, P nut, and so on.

Use the letters as shown in the photograph to make 'one-word' poems. Display the completed efforts on a large cut-out of the letter in question.

MINI-POEMS

A mini-poem should take no more than two lines, and relies for its effect on an understanding of image. The first line comes from the real world, something anyone could see by simply looking out of the window.

First lines might look like this:

Birds balancing on the telephone wires
or *Autumn leaves falling from the trees*
or *Snow whirling from a winter sky*

Choose one first line and put it on the board, for example:

Birds balancing on the telephone wires look like

music notes on a Christmas song sheet
churchgoers sitting in the pew
a queue of people waiting for a bus
the school choir at the carol concert.

Now lose the words 'look like' and a mini-poem is born.

Birds balancing on the telephone wires,
a queue of schoolchildren waiting for the bus.

Birds balancing on the telephone wires,
music notes on a Christmas song sheet.

Ask children to work in pairs, one child selecting a 'real world' starter (perhaps something that can be seen from the classroom window), the other making up the imaginary second line.
This technique also makes a good class or group lesson. Find a common starting line, for example:

Stars in the night sky look like

and ask each child to think of another 'looks like' line, and add it to the original. Make it a competition to see how many they can find. Some will be fairly pedestrian, others show a flash of insight.

For example,

nails hammered into the dark,
glitter scattered over a Christmas card,
sequins shining on a black dress,
drawing pins stuck into the blackboard,
goldfish swimming in a deep lake,
buttons sewn on a school blazer......

Drop the words 'look like' from the first line and, with the children's help, make the comparisons into a long image poem with pattern and rhythm.

Mini-poems with a common first line can be copied on to a cut-out, for example,

Autumn leaves falling from a tree - on a leaf shape; *Birds balancing on the telephone wires* - in silver pen on bird silhouette; *Stars in the night sky* - on star shapes against a black background.

(Children can produce their own autumn leaves, or commercially produced leaf shapes can be used – as shown in the photograph – to make a quick display.)

MINI-POSTER POEMS

Shape and mini-poems can be combined in an interesting way. First make up some rules to work to, perhaps no more than five words in a line, or four lines with only three words in each.

Turn the mini-poems into poster poems by drawing a wave-effect outline. Write the poem between the waves, so that the letters touch the lines, as shown in the photograph.

Full moon glows,
night breeze blows,
boats ride high,
shadowed waves sigh.

CONTRASTS

Even the very youngest non-writing children can tackle this idea. Take vividly contrasting themes, balancing one evenly with the other for effect. Think of *black and white, summer and winter, great and small, high and low,* and, for older children, *hope and despair, famine and plenty, lonely and one of a crowd,* and so on.

Day and night

Talk with the youngest children about what they can see in the street in the daytime. What about the street at night? Think of people and animals, of sounds and colours, how busy it is in the day, how quiet it is at night.

On the board, write two simple contrasting patterns, for example:

In the day..................
and...........................
along the busy street.

In the night........................
and...................................
along the lonely street.

Collect ideas from the children and demonstrate how they can make a poem from the pattern on the board. It might look like this:

In the day children race
and mothers push prams
along the busy street.

In the night cats prowl
and the policeman walks
along the lonely street.

In the day the sun shines
and people stroll
along the busy street.

In the night the moon glitters
and shadows dance
along the lonely street.

Let those children who are ready to write make up new poems using the pattern provided. More advanced writers may well wish to move on from this to produce poems with their own individual pattern.

The children can make simple-fold one-poem books with a verse on either side of the page. Using a pencil or crayons very lightly, shade behind the day poem in yellow, and behind night poems in grey or purple.

War and peace

Older children are often very involved in thinking about some of the deep concerns of the wider world. Contrast provides an effective way of helping them towards expressing their thoughts and ideas.
Use newspaper and magazine photographs to start off poems which deal with war. Find words and phrases to describe the sights and sounds, the feelings of people (with emphasis on the children) who are caught up in war. Brainstorm these ideas on the board, then look for contrasting images, words and phrases to do with peace.

The teacher may need to help children to find a starting point for this kind of poem. Look at the child's word list or initial brainstorming, and help him/her to choose an arresting image or a repeated sound with which to begin. Then suggest s/he contrasts the war image/sound with a peaceful one.

Sounds: gunfire, screaming, children crying
Sights: burning buildings, people running, soldiers, smoke
Smells: smoke, garbage
Images: ruins like broken blackened teeth
gunfire like a thunderstorm
smoke rising like wispy grey balloons
snipers crouching like children playing hide and seek

The child might begin her poem by collecting together some sounds:

Shells screaming, children crying,
soldiers shouting, mothers pleading,
sounds of war
fill the smoky skies.

She can use a similar format to introduce ideas of peace:

Seagulls screaming, children laughing,
waves splashing, fathers joking,
sounds of peace
fill the sunny skies... and so on.

Allow children to work at their own pace, using their own ideas, but always be ready to help them find starting points from their initial 'shopping list'. The use of contrasting peaceful sounds, sights, images, etc., emphasises the horror of a world at war.

Contrasting poems such as *war and peace, famine and plenty, pollution and a green environment, birth and death,* etc., are topics suited to the more sophisticated writer, but many children can use similar skills to tackle less demanding contrasts, for example: *light and dark, heat and cold, home and away, far and near,* etc.

THE LONGEST POEM IN THE WORLD

This is an excellent way of getting groups of children to work co-operatively on one poem. It is put together in a similar fashion to the old game of 'consequences'.

The first pair or group of children start the poem off by choosing two characters and a setting - perhaps,

Harry met Sally
down by the park.
Mum said, 'Listen kids,
be home before it's dark!'
But...........

The next group takes up the poem.

Billy's old granny
was tied to a tree.
She shouted to the children,
'Please help get me free!'
So...........

Sally said to Harry,
'Can we cut this rope?'
Harry's knife was blunt,
'With this?' he said. 'Some hope!'
And...........

This poetry saga can take several days to complete (if ever!). However, each group must stick to the rules: four lines only, lines 2 and 4 with an end-rhyme. It can be as zany as they like - in fact, the zanier, the better!

Pin up a roll of frieze paper and let the first group write out their verse on a sheet of A5 paper. They should paste it into place with their linking word – *but, so* or *and* – printed off to the right.
Then the next group continues, putting their four-line verse into position, and so on. This poetry task provides a lot of fun, both for the class members themselves and for children from the rest of the school, many of whom will be keen to read what happens next.

'FOUND' POEMS

'Found' poems are exactly what the name implies. These are poems which are made up from words which are all around, sometimes found in the strangest places! Think of the words and phrases on a coffee jar, *'This coffee has a rich full-bodied taste. Enjoy it black, white or with a swirl of cream to add a touch of luxury'*; or on a box of tea bags, *'Over 150 years of experience in the selection and blending of teas'*. Use some of the words from old letters, scraps of newsprint, recipes or, best of all perhaps, the magic promised in plant catalogues and on the backs of seed packets.
Let the children choose a seed packet, recipe or a coffee jar label. Ask them to cut out or copy a selection of words and phrases which they have found on the packet. They should rearrange these, adding words of their own choosing to make a new and exciting poem.

This poem, inspired by a seed packet, is by a ten-year-old:

Summer spectacular

Salpiglossis carnival
mixed. Promises are
painted on the packet.

Rip open foil. Pepper
the ground with seeds
and wait for the sun.

Come July. Bold colours,
scarlet, orange and gold,
blaze like a forest fire.

Moira Andrew's poem 'Raspberry jam' was based on phrases found in a recipe book

SECRETS

The secret life of coal

This topic is particularly suited to places where there is a history of mining. Collect some lumps of coal and let the children look at, touch and smell the coal as it is passed from hand to hand. On the board, make a shopping list of descriptive words and images.

> *black as jet,*
> *shiny as a cat's eyes,*
> *black as a winter's night,*
> *smells like old pennies,*
> *coloured like spilled oil, etc.*

The children should make up their own shopping list, perhaps using the 'borrow one, find one' technique. When they are ready to write, they should put their ideas together to make a picture in words for someone who has never seen coal before.

Then ask them to think of the secrets hidden beneath the dusty black outer skin: *the long-dead forests which made the coal deposits, the darkness from which it was hewn, the dangers faced by miners in bringing it to the surface, the heat and light and colour in a coal fire.*

From these 'secrets', the children are able to move on from straight description to less tangible ideas.

Coal

Black as jet,
Yet shiny as glass
It glitters in the sun.
It has smooth sides,
Worn away by erosion.
It smells musty, as dusty
As roads in summer.
Made from trees felled
Long, long ago.
Inside the shell of black
Hides a secret.
The roaring and leaping
Of smoke and sparks
Ready to burst into life.

Angharad Whitfield (10)

Coal

Black as the night,
sparkling like gems,
rainbow colours caught inside.
It smells like old metal,
feels as rough as a cave wall.
It took years to form,
days to extract,
hours to shovel,
minutes to burn.
The fire, the heat, the smoke
caught under the skin.
The embers glow as it dies
to smouldering grey ash.

Richard Jones (10)

Write the poems inside 'opening' books made of black card which have been cut into rough coal shapes. Decorate the writing with red, yellow and orange flames, using pencil crayon **(see photograph above).**

To make an effective display of these 'coal' books, arrange them on a fire collage of metallic and coloured paper flames.

TREASURE CHEST

Younger children enjoy the idea of finding a long-hidden treasure chest. Either use a picture or mock up a box as a dusty, cobwebby chest. Ask the children to make up a scenario for it: where it was unearthed, by whom, etc. Perhaps it was a mariner's chest. If so, think about the treasures that might be stored inside, unseen for many years.

Make a 'shopping list' of ideas: *jewels, pearls, guns, coins, maps.* Let the children look for adjectives and verbs to go with their treasure, and add to either side of the list. They might enjoy making it into a simple number poem:

Inside the pirate chest
we found,
ten red rubies shining,
nine white pearls gleaming,
eight precious coins sparkling,
seven green emeralds winking,
six silver spiders spinning,
five lacy fans crumbling,
four feather pens rusting,
three wicked masks grinning,
two dangerous guns popping
and
one ancient map
marked with an X

Display the poems inside an opening treasure chest shape, lavishly decorated with gems, pearls, coins, etc. Use foil paper or pasta painted over with silver and gold to make the jewels spilling from the chest.

LADDER POEMS

This starter is perhaps a word game rather than a poem in the true sense, but is of considerable value in encouraging a word-search. The challenge which it poses appeals to the older children, although the task is more difficult than they anticipate.

Begin with a compound word, such as *butterfly* or *wallflower*, or a two-word noun, such as *tennis court* or *market stall*. The trick is to get back to the original starter always using a recognised word or phrase.
For example:

wallflower
flower pot
pot black
blackball
ball boy
boyfriend
friendship
shipshape
shape up
up market
market garden
garden wall
wallflower

overall
all out
outlaw
lawman
mankind
kind heart
heartbreak
breakwater
waterfall
fall over
overall

HEADLINES

Make a collection of headlines from newspapers. Try to find those with creative possibilities, for example: *Forgotten island, Back to the twilight zone, Flight of fear, A many-splendoured thing, The craziness of a smart fox, Looking back, Wheel of fortune,* and so on.

Let the children each choose a headline as a title for a poem. Suggest that they use their word-listing and brain-storming skills to work out an individual response to the headline. These make very varied poems and allow the children a measure of autonomy in their writing.

Headlines make an excellent 'end-on' activity, that is, something on which children can choose to work in their own time - after completing another set task, for example. Vary the headlines used (a new batch every week, perhaps), pasting them across black card pinned above the writing area. Suggest that the children display and decorate the poems as they like - in frames, one-poem books or inside a decorative border.

WHAT IS IN THE BOX?

This idea is a sure-fire starter for six and seven-year-olds. Group the children on the carpet and let them look at a small decorated box. Suggest that a tiny creature lives inside the box. Ask what makes his home different from theirs – *size, shape, colour - no doors and no windows!* Suggest that the creature might be magic. This creates great interest among the children.

Put the box aside and tell the children that they are going to play a guessing game. Ask them to guess some creatures which are small enough to live in the little box. Write six of the children's suggestions in a list *in the middle* of the board.

Now move to the left and ask for ideas about colour/pattern, etc. (Remember, this is a magic creature - no ordinary *black ants* – perhaps *purple, turquoise* or *silver* ants!) Moving to the right side, list ways of moving: *running, skipping, scurrying, jogging,* etc.

Don't go for the first words suggested - get the children to explore the possibilities. This oral work goes a long way to extending the children's knowledge of and interest in language. Now 'top and tail' the poem, asking the question, *What is in the box? Is it......*

Finish with a phrase such as, *We don't know. Let's look!*

What is in the box?

Is it
a silver ant scurrying?
a golden beetle jogging?
a zigzag ladybird singing?
a purple tadpole swimming?
a luminous slug slithering?
a fragile dragonfly floating?
We don't know.
Let's look!

It is a good idea to colour-code the children's ideas as you scribe them on the board, for example, using red for nouns, green for adjectives, blue for verbs, etc. For children who are just beginning to write their own poems, suggest that they choose four 'red words' (creatures), four 'green words' (describing words) and four 'blue words' (how the creatures move). This method enables the children to make up four lines for themselves. Help them to 'top and tail' the lines and, hey presto, an instant poem!

Experienced writers can choose their own set of words. Encourage them to top and tail the poems as they think best. Copy the finished poems into an opening box shape, as shown in the photograph below.

(Don't forget to let the children into the secret of the box - as if they would let you! I use a model spider with waving legs.)

This pattern can be used to good effect for many different topics.
Who is hiding in the hedge? What is in the magic purse? Who is behind the magic door?

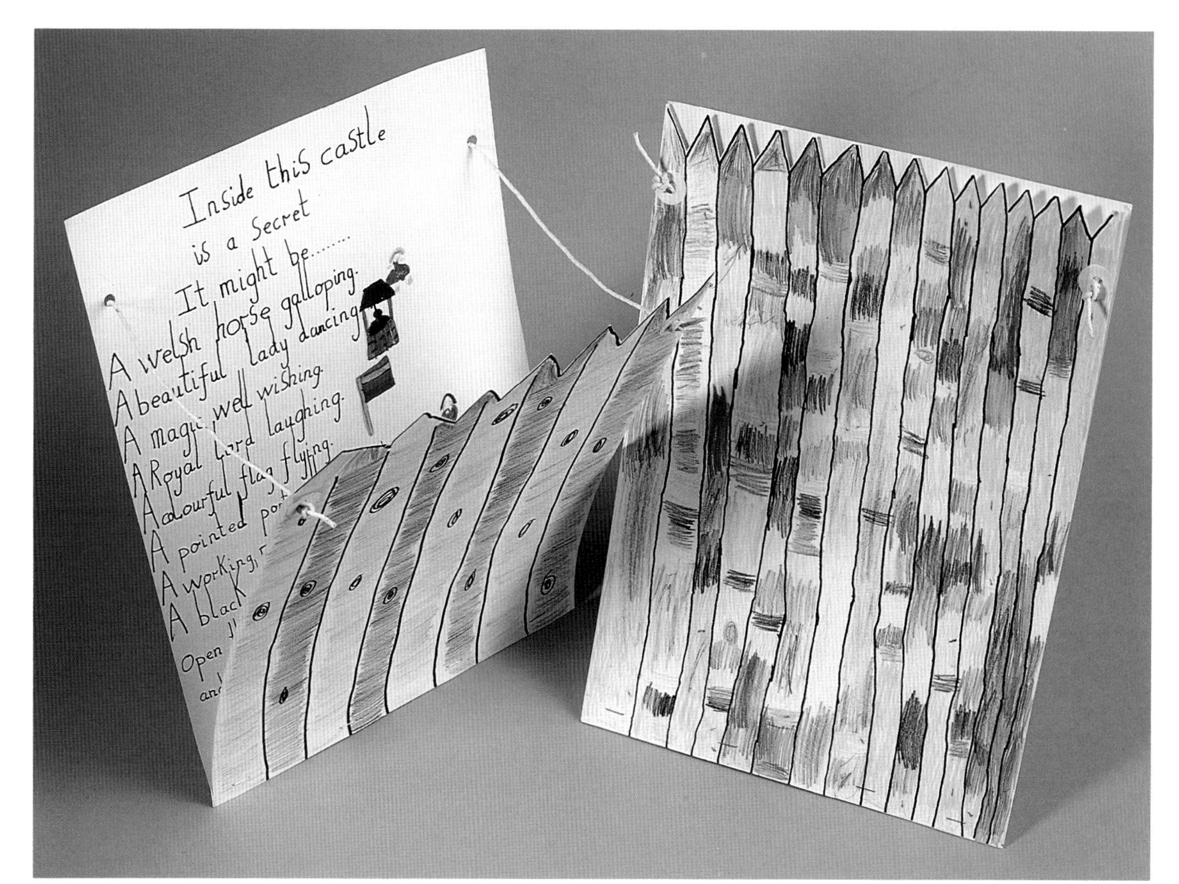

Children who had been on a castle visit adapted the pattern and asked **Who is behind the drawbridge?** *Is it.........a jolly jester laughing? a beautiful lady spinning? a brave knight jousting?* and so on.

BOX OF DREAMS

Older children can use the idea of the box starter to produce some very sophisticated poems: *Box of dreams, Box of nightmares, Box of wishes, Box of sounds, Box of colours,* etc.

Suggest that the box might contain untold treasures and ask the children to write down their ideas in lines, topping and tailing as they think best.

Box of wishes

In the box of wishes
where mists swirl
and magic lurks
a magician hides our wishes.
Dreams of mountains,
dreams of rainbows,
dreams of starlight,
dreams of summer,
are all locked up
with the wishes
of the world.
And there they hide
until they are granted
and the dreams
of the world
come true at last.

Rebecca Carter (9)

Box of dreams

On my table,
beside my bed
is a little wooden box
all green and gold,
all gold and red
decorated with
leaves and trees.
In the morning
I wake up
with lots of dreams
stored in my head.
I fold them up
all neat and straight
and place them
in the little wooden box
until night comes to
paint the sky with stars.

Lily Devine (10)

Display the poems inside box shapes - round, square, rectangular. Use gold and silver pens and a great deal of colour to make very decorative opening lids for the poems. Collect a variety of interesting boxes and place on a table beneath the poetry display.

WHEELS

Poems about wheels can add a new dimension to a topic on transport. Ask the children to listen to the sounds made by different kinds of wheels and to imitate, then write out, the 'songs' they make. Use this song as a chorus to a wheels poem. For example,

The children can put together words to describe the train, pram, bicycle, tractor, racing car, 'old banger', etc. They should think about what it looks like, how it moves, where it is going, the people involved, and so on.

Think of other places where wheels are important - a mine shaft, Big Ben, the fairground, a traction engine, the inside of a clock or pocket watch. Listen to the rhythms, look at the way the wheels move and make rhythmic poems with their own chorus.

Write out the finished wheels poems in the round. To complete the display, arrange on a table below a collection of wheels and books and poems about transport.

Weather wheel

Wheels can be used for sequential poems related to the seasons, months of the year, days of the weeks, times of the day, and so on.
Read Moira Andrew's poem, 'Weather wheel' **(see page 2)**, and work on a similar poem with the children. Think of the weather at each season of the year, what clothes the children wear, what games they play, etc. List these ideas on the board, making it into a group poem.

Another idea is to think of fruit and flowers, colour in the garden, a tree through the seasons, spawn to frog, egg to butterfly, etc., and to arrange the words, phrases and ideas in a similar sequential way inside a wheel shape.
Encourage the children to work individually on their own version of a seasons poem. When they are satisfied with their rough work, let them draw around a teaplate, writing their spring, summer, autumn and winter lines in the appropriate segment. They could decorate around the edge with seasonal flowers and fruit.

THE POCKET WATCH

With the children sitting round you, show them an unfamiliar object (such as a pocket watch) wrapped up in a handkerchief. Suggest that you know that they will know what the object is, but no-one must tell! Hand the wrapped object to one child and ask her to find one word to describe how it feels - *hard, round, slippery, shiny, heavy.*
Pass the object on and let the next child find a different word. This becomes more difficult as the game progresses. List these words on the board. After five or six turns, ask the children to think in terms of image:

as hard as a stone/rock/brick
as round as a pound coin/a medal/the moon
as slippery as ice/glass/a polished floor

Now undo the handkerchief to show what the object is. Look for words and phrases to describe the look of it – *ancient, precious, silver* – again asking each child for one word. Where possible, extend the images as before:
ancient as my grandad....ancient as a treasure....ancient as the pyramids

Using the pocket watch as an example, open it up and ask the children to suggest what it looks like – *an opening flower, a shell, a silver butterfly.*

If there is an inscription, ask a child to read it aloud. This may add to the history of the object. Ask the children to think about who first owned it, what might have happened to it, where it was hidden, and so on. List all the ideas on the board.
(The inscription on the pocket watch reads:

John Halliday
Died in France of wounds
1.5.17

Using part of the inscription makes it a 'found poem'.)

Show the children how those ideas and images can be put together to make a poem which not only describes the look and feel of the object, but gives a flavour of the personal history behind it. The group poem below was put together in this way, piece by piece.

The widow's watch

Smooth as a pebble,
hard and heavy,
cold as winter.
The widow's watch
opens like a dove's wings
silver in the sun.
In memory of John Halliday
died in France of wounds
one bright day in May.

For those children who are experienced writers, arrange a collection of historical artefacts and let them choose what they would like to write about (see photograph on page 22). Suggest that the children use a similar method to that indicated for the pocket watch.

RIDDLES AND PUZZLE POEMS

Riddles are image poems turned inside-out. Children enjoy the element of guessing that is inherent in riddles, and are usually very keen to try out their word-puzzles on other members of the class. In these circumstances, there is seldom a problem in getting young writers to read their work aloud.

To introduce the idea of writing riddles, use the board to make up a simple image poem. Work on a format which the children have used previously, for example:

The sun is like a yellow balloon
floating in the summer sky.
The sun is like a golden frisbee
whizzing over the highest trees.

Now show how *'The sun is like'* can be altered to *'I am like'* so that the poem now reads:

I am like a yellow balloon
floating in the summer sky.
I am like a golden frisbee
whizzing over the highest trees.

Add a question:
What am I?

What is the sun?

The sun is a yellow balloon
drifting behind the hill.
It is an amber frisbee
skimming through the air.

The sun is an orange Smartie
squidging between the clouds.
It is a golden pancake
flicked into outer space.

The sun is a dandelion
swaying in the breeze.
It is a sunflower
stretching up to Heaven.

Use the front cover as a title page called, perhaps, *Riddle of the sea.* Illustrate with pictures of, for example, a sea-horse, a whale, a fishing boat, a seagull, etc., so that the reader has to work out the answer to the question *What am I?* Write the poem on page 2 and construct an opening flap on page 3. The answer (for example, *I am a fishing boat*) should be written out or drawn beneath the flap.

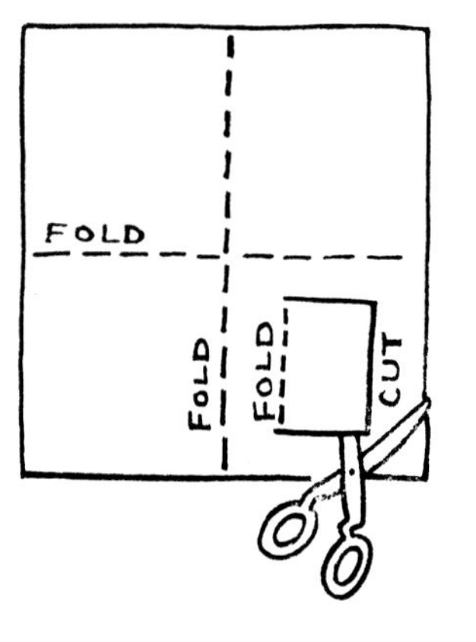

Weather Riddles

This topic provides an easy entry into writing and guessing riddles - as illustratred on the facing page. Children from about six upwards can work on a weather theme, for example, suggesting animals for the wind. The first lines of their riddles may look like this: *I am like a fierce lion/ I am like a gentle butterfly/ I can howl like a wolf,* etc. Riddles should finish with a question in the last line: *What am I?* or, away from the animal image, for older children:

I am as invisible as a ghost.
I am as cold as winter.
I can whisper in the forest.
I can scream across the waves.
I can live on the mountain tops.
I can whistle in the streets.
What am I?

The children can describe fog, mist, a storm, rain, thunder, hail, clouds, lightning, and so on. This can lead to a question and answer sequence for parents' evenings or for a children's session in assembly.

Riddles of place

Riddles can be introduced into environmental topics based on where the children live. Ten-year-olds in Penarth (near Cardiff) wrote about the local church, their own school, the distinctive town clock, the pier, the promenade.

Riddle of Penarth

I am the colour of aquamarine,
I am like clouds on a wet day.
I am as luscious as the grass.
I am like a silk tablecloth,
sometimes I wrinkle,
sometimes I crease.
I carry many burdens
on my back.
I hold a feast every day.
I tie with blue ribbons
and green threads.
What am I? *(answer: I am the sea)*
Katherine

To work on this kind of poem, suggest that children concentrate on something very specific, peculiar to their own particular area – a building, a street, a lake, the hills, etc. To display the riddles, pin the poems (correctly placed) to a simplified plan of the locality. Add local books and photographs to the display.

If you take the children on an educational outing - to a museum, a nature walk or farm visit - make riddle-writing an option to give variety alongside the more usual poem or piece of descriptive writing.

Machines

Machines - diggers, cranes, tractors, etc. - provide excellent topics for riddle-writing. Children can describe diggers as dinosaurs, a crane as a pterodactyl, a tractor as a dragon, and so on.

Let the youngest children make riddles from transport pictures and photographs: trains, aeroplanes, helicopters, yachts, etc. For example:

I am like a white butterfly
fluttering across the waves.
What am I?

(I am a boat)

I am like a dragonfly
with spinning wings
hovering in the summer air.
What am I?

(I am a helicopter)

For those children who are not yet writing, ask an adult to act as scribe from their dictation. The children can copy out their riddles, then get the others to try to match pictures to poems.

Animals

Use a similar technique with animal pictures and photographs, getting the children to use their emerging powers of description to make a simple riddle-poem, for example:

I wear a red coat
with black buttons.
I am as small as
a baby's thumb nail
but I can fly and I can climb
What am I?

(I am a ladybird)

I shine like a jewel.
I flash across the pond
like an underwater firework.
I twist and turn, hiding
in forests of green weed.
Now you see me, now you don't.
What am I?

(I am a goldfish)

As before, the children can hide the pictures beneath a flap. This makes an interesting wall display answering the question – *What am I?*

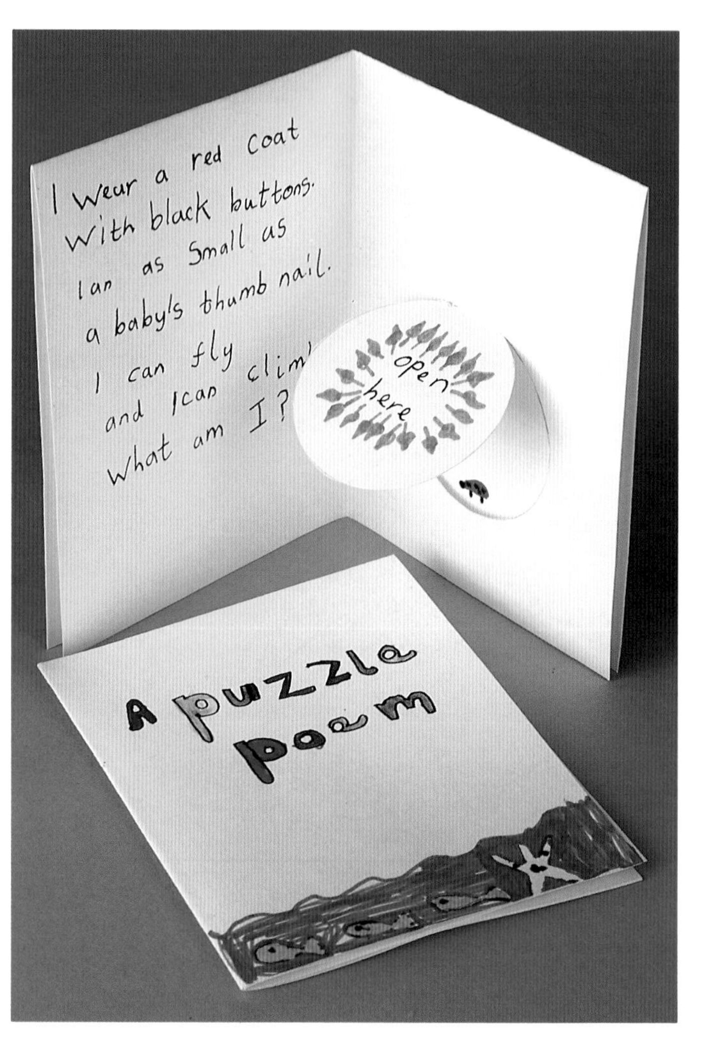

The elements

The poetry of the elements can be linked to work on science and technology. Ask the children to choose one of the elements, brainstorming *fire/earth/water/air* words. Look for images of colour, touch, movement, sound, etc., so that they build up a list of ideas, for example:

Fire looks like a field of poppies, sunset painting the sky red
Fire sounds like the roaring of dinosaurs, like the moaning of the wind
Fire feels like a dragon's tongue, red feathers tickling the coal
Fire moves like the incoming tide, an army marching
Fire smells like trolls' breath, sausages burning on a barbecue

They can then put together a riddle poem from these ideas - and more will flow as they work. Suggest that they do the same for the other elements. These riddles can be written as individual, group or class poems.

For a most impressive display, cut out large circles, painting or layering with papers in appropriate colours: all the browns and sand colours for earth; blues, greens and silver for water; pale blues and greys with white streaks for air; all the reds, yellows and oranges for fire. Write in felt-tip pen, or paste copies of the poems on the circles to hang from the ceiling as element mobiles.
(If there is a problem with mobiles setting off an alarm, pin the circles to a background frieze to make an equally effective wall display.)

Puzzle poems

A traditional type of riddle is made by hiding letters of the alphabet in the lines of a poem. This is more difficult for the children to attempt, but they will enjoy working out the answer. Suggest that the children try to find examples of this kind of riddle in their anthologies. They can copy them out, then try to make up one for themselves.

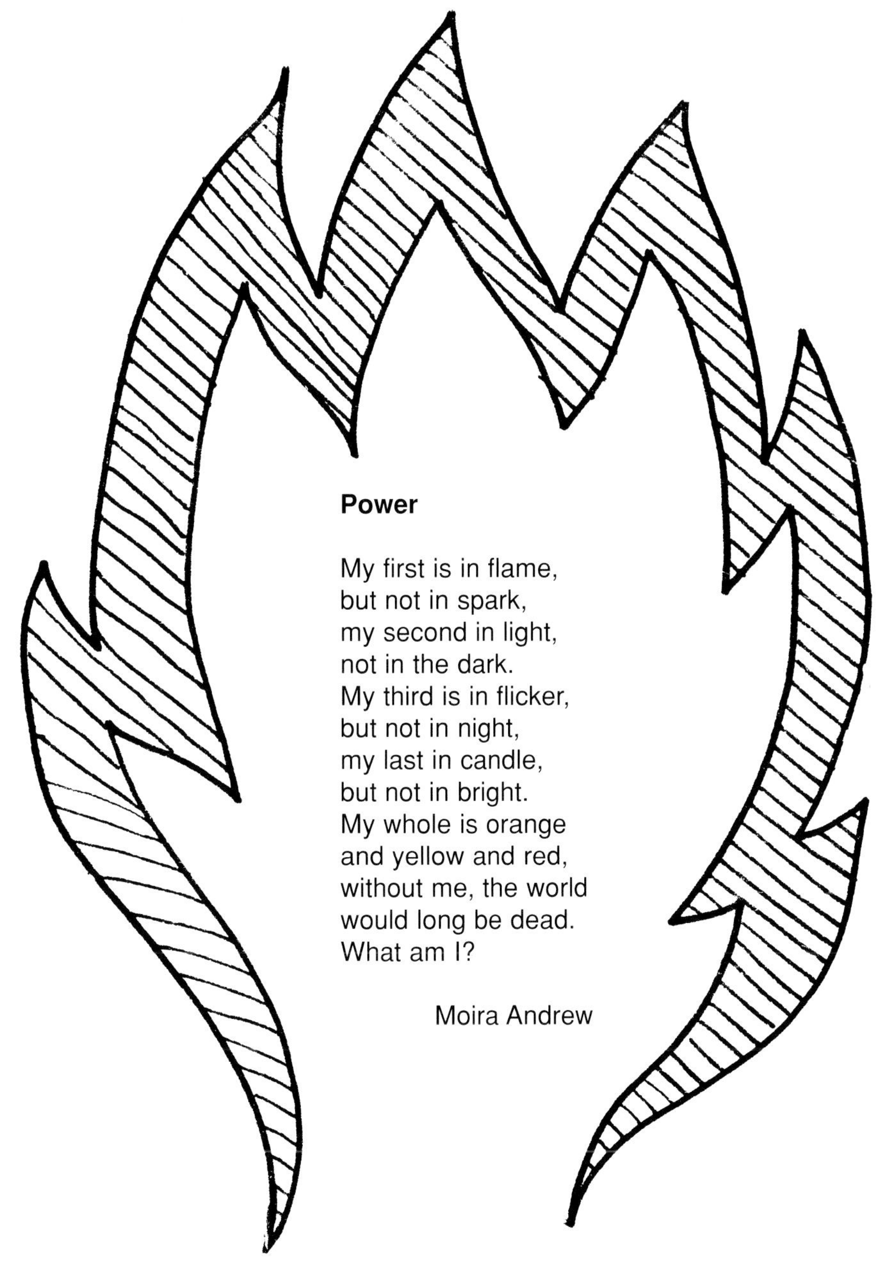

Power

My first is in flame,
but not in spark,
my second in light,
not in the dark.
My third is in flicker,
but not in night,
my last in candle,
but not in bright.
My whole is orange
and yellow and red,
without me, the world
would long be dead.
What am I?

Moira Andrew

Show the children how to work out the answer. For example, the first letter is one which is found in the word FLAME, but not in SPARK. The letter 'A' is automatically cancelled out, being common to both words, so the first letter of the mystery word is F, L, M or E.....and so on. (Put together, the hidden letters spell out the element which is described in the last four lines - FIRE).

KENNINGS

A kenning is a way of describing something which tells you what it is, or sounds like, but does not use the simple word for that thing. For example, thunder might be *a cloud-basher*, wind *a hat-snatcher*, water a *fire-drowner*, and so on.

Writing kennings makes an excellent class exercise. Once the children realise what is needed, there is no stopping them! A class of six-year-olds produced the kennings below - and they could have made them much longer if time and space on the board had allowed.

a tree-tearer
a bin-basher
a window-rattler
a roof-destroyer
a slate-thrower
a cat-frightener
a traffic-stopper
a river-riser
a wave-tosser
a boat-drowner

What is it?

a garden-painter
a tree-whitener
a fence-topper
a grass-icer
a car-hider
a traffic-silencer
a road-coverer
a snowman-maker
an ear-chiller
a nose-reddener

What is it?

It is helpful to put the title on the board or on their rough work to remind the children what they are describing. Suggest that they find ten (or 20, or whatever, but give them a goal) different kennings, then write it out with the title deleted to make a puzzle-poem.

Use a tall one-poem book to write out the kennings, giving answers on the back page beneath flaps, as before **(see line drawing above).**

THROUGH THE DOOR

Many poets have used the idea of looking on the other side of a door, a window or through a gateway. Sometimes they think of what life might be like on the other side. Sometimes they visualise gardens, and sometimes a fantasy world.

Young children can write about how they feel safe and warm indoors on a winter's day, how cold and lonely it can be outside in the street. Ask them to write an *Inside/outside* poem, copying the first and third lines, as suggested:

I am inside, looking outside
at the falling snow.
I am outside, looking inside
at the firelight glow.

I am inside, looking outside
at the pouring rain.
I am outside, looking inside
through the window pane.

It is often better, however, to avoid asking the children to use rhyme. From their ideas, make a list of things they can see from the window on a wet/snowy/sunny day, or a list of sounds on a windy day, such as:

dustbin lids rattling,
car tyres whooshing,
flower pots rolling,
wet washing flapping....and so on.

Now find lines with which to 'top and tail' the poem. Let the children write their own version of the poem, borrowing two ideas from the group list and finding two or more of their own.

Stormy day

I am inside, looking outside,
listening to the bitter wind,
dustbin lids rattling,
flower pots rolling,
ancient trees creaking,
shed door squeaking,
rusty gates clattering,
dead leaves blowing
lonely footsteps running.
Listening to the bitter wind,
I am inside, looking outside.

Write the inside/outside poems in an opening 'window'. Using coloured pencil with a light touch, show a child's face looking out, drawn beneath the writing.

To begin work on a *Through the door* poem, ask the children to make two lists, one a list of ordinary things: *mums pushing prams, people queueing at the bus stop, cars speeding along the road.* Then get them to make a fantasy list, things that would give them a tremendous surprise if they should see them on the pavement outside: *a dragon breathing fire, a giant in seven-league boots, an alien stepping out of a flying saucer.* Now suggest that they write a poem using these contrasting ideas of real and fantasy worlds.

Go and open the door.
Perhaps you'll see
mums pushing prams,
a crowd at the bus stop.....
Or maybe you'll see
a fire-breathing dragon,
an alien in a flying saucer....
But don't be afraid.
Go and open the door.

Some of the children can add further verses, still keeping to the pattern outlined. This time they could suggest *Perhaps you'll hear,* again contrasting reality and fantasy. (This is a 'copycat' pattern based on 'The Door' by Miroslav Holub.)

Imagine standing by a door in an old crumbling wall. Imagine that passing through that door leads to enchantment and a land of magic, for example, *an underwater garden, the way to the stars, a jungle landscape, land of trolls/giants/unicorns,* etc. (based on 'Through that door' by John Cotton).

Through that door
Is a desert island,
Where pirates prowl
And mermaids sing,
Where, ten fathoms deep,
In a sunken wreck
Lie human bones and
Coins of purest gold.

Through that door
Is an enchanted garden,
Where...................

Through that door
Is a crumbling castle,
Where...................

Display this kind of writing inside an opening door, using an A4 frame big enough to accommodate the child's writing.
The poem should be written out in the middle of one sheet overlaid by a top sheet into which is cut the opening door.

Make a class display of door poems by painting a fantasy street scene on frieze paper and pinning individual door poems into place along 'the street', as shown below.

PORTRAIT OF A TREE

This is more of a picture-poem than a true poem. It was the result of looking closely at a particular tree, drawing the general shape quickly, then making comments about each section in turn; nettles and daisies growing around the roots, the breeze ruffling leaves in the topmost branches, and so on.

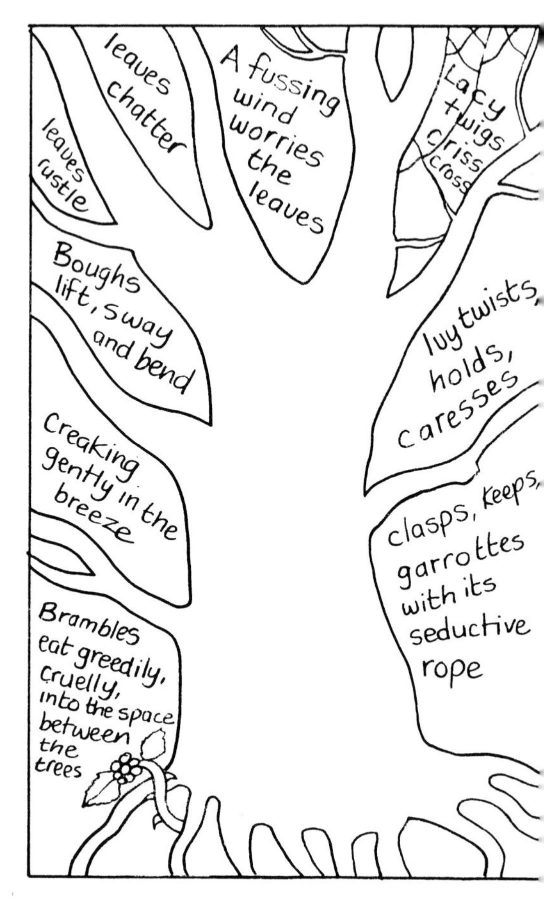

To copycat this kind of poem (see page 41), take the children into the school grounds or the local park. Ask them to choose an interestingly-shaped tree. They should draw its general outline, then make notes on things they see or hear at each level: birds nesting, leaves rustling, squirrels scampering, branches creaking, etc. Suggest that they use image - *'Daisies like slender-fingered hands'*, and list tree-words - *'leaf, twig, branch, bough, trunk, roots'*. Suggest that the words the children write are as much a portrait of the tree as the sketch itself.

This can also be used as a group poem, especially where children find difficulty in putting words on paper. Ask each group to make up one mini-poem. If the children are very young, the teacher can scribe these ideas, writing them out in best in place on a painted tree on the classroom wall.

Use this method to make a group poem to describe other outside visits, for example, a visit to a castle, the harbour, a nature trail, etc. Older, more confident children, will enjoy making these portrait-poems individually.

POEMS FROM PICTURES

Posters and paintings can provide a rich source of starter ideas for poetry-writing. Choose a poster or a picture which has some mystery about it, not one which reveals all at first glance.

Poster poems

Put a poster up where everyone can see it easily. Ask the children to look at it silently for a minute or two. Suggest that they explore the colours and shapes, consider what sounds they might hear if they were part of the scene. Ask them to think about how they would feel if they were trapped inside the frame.

Now ask the children to respond orally, making a group 'shopping list' from their ideas on the board. Use only two suggestions for each category - colours, sounds, feelings, for example - but encourage the children to express as many ideas as possible orally. This means that when they come to make their own individual shopping list, they have a great many options to choose from. Suggest that the less experienced writers use the 'borrow one, find one' technique (see page 4), to get their list going.

Use two facing blank pages, the one on the left for the shopping list of ideas, the one on the right for the first rough version of the poem. Suggest to the children that they cross ideas off their list as they use them. Suggest that the children look for images and connections in the picture. In the jungle poster which stimulated the poems shown below, the children found: *a giant butterfly looking like a grounded plane, creepers twining like snakes round the tree trunks, a clump of reeds like a crown of thorns, a panther's eyes glaring like spotlights...*

Suggest that a way into the poems might be to gather all the sounds, colours or feelings together, for example:

Roaring, hissing, splashing water.....

Tigers roaring, water splashing,
cats whining, trees creaking.....

The dense jungle is bright
with greens, yellows, reds.....

No mention here of the 'One day.....', 'Once upon a time.....' beginning. This approach is best left for story-writing!

The poster shows a number of different animals meeting at a water hole. The sun is high and bright as a ripe tangerine, and a number of the children used this as a key marker, both in their poems and the linked artwork.

Many of the children considered what it would feel like to be trapped in such a forest. Suggest that the children's poems end in the jungle itself. Deborah finishes with a despairing question, *'Will I ever get out?'*

This work looks at its best displayed within its own cut-out frame. Ask the children to write the finished poem in best in the middle of an A4 sheet, leaving plenty of space around it. Cover with another A4 sheet and mark around the poem shape with a pencil. Work on the top sheet only, making it into a colourful jungle/seascape/forest, or whatever. Cut out the hole only after the artwork is completed, and carefully paste the top sheet so that the poem shows through the hole. The children may wish to edge the poem shape with one line of coloured pencil or felt-tip marker.

Display a group of poems together and add overlapping cut-out leaf shapes, animals, or sea creatures for an all-over forest/underwater/jungle effect.

This poem and its picture were inspired by a poster showing a bleak winter landscape where a wolf is howling at the moon

Postcard poems

A collection of postcards of paintings is a wonderful investment. Let the children have enough time to choose a postcard which appeals to them, one which is full of excitement or adventure, of fun or mystery.

Ask the children to imagine standing just outside the postcard. What would the weather be like? What might they hear, smell or feel? What voices might they be able to listen to? What secrets are hidden inside the frame?

Some children might wish to describe the scene as a mini-poem or in haiku format. The description should be so clear and accurate that someone unable to see the postcard could imagine it.

Below, two ten-year-olds give their different versions of David Hockney's painting, 'Beach Umbrella'.

Beach scene

One long shadow
stretching across the sand
like a dark speeding arrow.

The sea
a clear bright blue, calm
as cream in a dish.

Furrows in the sand
where a thousand burning feet
have passed.

Caroline Conder

A hot summer's day

Shadow
Soft sand
Long thin pole
Bright basic colours
Sun umbrella
Shade

Sarah Dawes

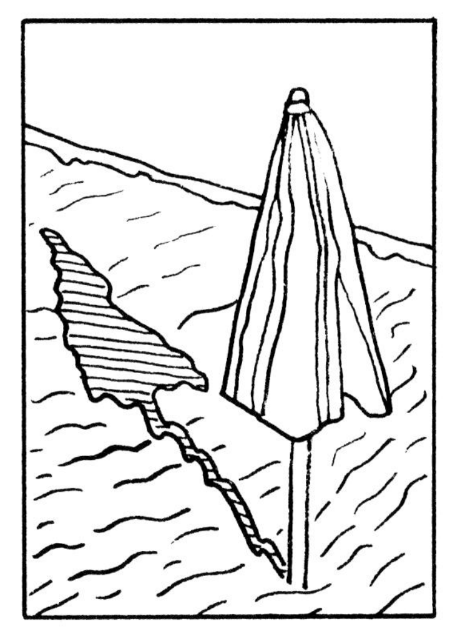

These poems convey some of the heat and colour which the artist has put into his painting. They echo the shapes *(long thin pole, shadow/like a dark speeding arrow)* and would almost make it possible for someone to paint a copy of the Hockney picture simply by reading the poems.

To begin this kind of work on postcard poems, suggest that the children first follow the 'shopping list' principle to rough out their poems. They should try to get rid of unnecessary words - look at the economy in 'A hot summer's day'.

Find a variety of postcards so that the children have a choice of scene - sea scenes, countryside, storms, portraits, etc., and give them a choice of artist, so that different moods and colours are reflected in the subsequent poems.

Thomas (9) looked hard and long at Matisse's *Le violoniste à la fenêtre* which shows only the back of the figure. He told me he thought it was one of the saddest pictures he had ever seen. Here is his poem:

The violinist

He scrapes the bow,
the music is slow, high
as the sailing clouds.
He thinks of his father
lying lost and cold,
deep underground.
The music echoes
like a thin song
on a silver ribbon,
reaching from father
to son and back.

Put the finished poems inside frames and hang them, gallery-fashion, alongside the original postcards.

For details of further Belair publications,
please write to: Libby Masters,
BELAIR PUBLICATIONS LIMITED,
Albert House, Apex Business Centre,
Boscombe Road, Dunstable, LU5 4RL.

For sales and distribution in North America and South America,
INCENTIVE PUBLICATIONS,
3835 Cleghorn Avenue, Nashville, Tn 37215.
USA.

For sales and distribution in Australia
EDUCATIONAL SUPPLIES PTY LTD
8 Cross Street, Brookvale, NSW 2100.
Australia

For sales and distribution (in other territories)
FOLENS PUBLISHERS
Albert House, Apex Business Centre,
Boscombe Road, Dunstable, LU5 4RL.
United Kingdom.
E-mail: folens@folens.com